HAVE you ever found yourself **SCRATCHING** your head, **wondering** how to tell a WIZARD from a warlock?

CONTENTS

→ INTRODUCTION

Have you ever found yourself scratching your head, wondering how to tell a WIZARD from a WARLOCK, or a MONKEY from an APE? Or debating with your friends whether there's any difference between RAINFORESTS and JUNGLES?

You already know that there are definitely differences between things like plants and animals, and stalactites and stalagmites ... but what are they, exactly?

At last, you can stop frowning in puzzlement, because here are the answers to all the 'what's the difference?' questions you've ever thought of (and some you probably haven't). As well as all that, you can find out hundreds of other fascinating pieces of information: the biggest (and smallest) cities in the world, the five different types of rhinoceros alive today, and some headache cures you probably won't want to try – however bad your headache (or migraine) is.

If you've ever wanted to know the difference between a newt and a salamander, or if you'd like to find out how to get a metallic sheen on your teeth (and why you'd want to), read on ...

WHAT'S THE DIFFERENCE BETWEEN A FROG AND A TOAD?

This is an essential question to answer – there'd be no point in kissing a toad, after all.

Frogs and toads are both the same type of creature, called 'Anura' in Latin. The common name for Anura is frogs, so all toads are really frogs – but toads come under a separate family group from other frogs, so not all frogs are toads.

FROGS ...

... have smooth, slimy skin.
... have long, powerful back legs.
... lay their eggs in clusters.

TOADS ...

... have thicker, drier skin, which means they can be away from water for longer than frogs can.
... have shorter back legs than frogs, which means they tend to walk rather than hop.
... lay their eggs in chains.

To make things even more confusing, there are exceptions. Some frogs are commonly known as toads, and one member of the toad group is commonly known as a 'harlequin frog'.

Warty toads

You may have heard that toads can give you warts — but that's not true. Warts are caused by a viral infection, which isn't carried by toads. People probably made the toad-wart connection because of the warty-looking growths on a toad's skin. But these are actually glands that produce poison, to help defend toads from predators.

Deadly frogs

The most poisonous creature on Earth is the golden poison frog, which lives in the Columbian rainforest. The frogs are roughly 5 centimetres long and each one has just a milligram of poison on its skin — but that is still enough to kill several people. There is only one creature that can eat the golden poison frog — a snake that has developed some immunity to its poison. Anything else that eats one will certainly die.

Frog skin

Frogs shed their skin every week or so, pulling it over their heads just as you might take off a jumper. Usually, they eat it afterwards.

WHAT'S THE DIFFERENCE BETWEEN A POND AND A LAKE?

It's a common problem: you have a large body of water in the vast grounds of your mansion, and you're not sure whether to call it a lake or a pond. After all, you don't want to seem boastful.

Most people would agree that a pond is smaller than a lake. But by how much? And how else can you tell a lake from a pond? Unfortunately, there's no clear answer – but here are some rough guidelines:

PONDS ...

... are shallow enough for sunlight to reach the bottom, even in the deepest parts.
... are a similar temperature from top to bottom.
... have no waves on the shoreline.
... are shallow enough for water plants with roots to grow, even in the deepest parts.

LAKES ...

... are too deep in some places for sunlight to reach the bottom.
... are much colder at the bottom than at the top during summer.
... have a windswept shoreline where waves often lap.
... are too deep in places for water plants to grow.

What about size? It's the most obvious difference between a pond and a lake, but unfortunately no one can agree on an exact definition. Some organizations say that a pond can be a maximum of eight hectares – more than ten football pitches – some say five hectares, and others say two. By anybody's standards though, two hectares – nearly three football pitches – is pretty big.

Of course, there are exceptions. In New England, in the USA, large bodies of water are known as Great Ponds. The largest of them is nearly 3,500 hectares.

Here's one final difference to help you decide: lakes tend to have names, while ponds don't. If you think yours is a lake and not a pond, why not give it a name?

LARGE LAKE OR SMALL SEA?

The biggest area of enclosed water on Earth is the Caspian Sea at about 395,000 km^2. Sometimes it's described as the world's biggest lake, but of course that depends on the difference between a sea and a lake and it turns out that just like with ponds and lakes, there's no definite answer to that question either. The Michigan-Huron Lake is the largest lake in the world at roughly 117 km^2 - unless you count Michigan-Huron as two separate lakes. In that case, Lake Superior, at about 82,000 km^2, is the largest lake. And Lake Superior is definitely just one lake, and definitely not a sea - phew!

WHAT'S THE DIFFERENCE BETWEEN A FRUIT AND A VEGETABLE?

Which of these is the odd one out?

tomato

raspberry

pumpkin

aubergine

broccoli

cucumber

If you think raspberry is the odd one out, because it's a fruit and the rest are vegetables, you're wrong. Broccoli is actually the odd one out – it's the only one that ISN'T a fruit. Want to know why? Look away now if you're squeamish: a fruit is the ripe 'ovary' of a plant – that's the female reproductive bit – containing seed that has the potential to grow into a new plant. Tomatoes, cucumbers, pumpkins, aubergines, courgettes and peppers are technically all fruits. But ...

The word vegetable is used to describe any plant that's grown to eat, no matter which part of the plant is eaten ... unless of course it's a fruit. Unlike the word fruit, vegetable doesn't have a precise definition.

If you were a botanist – a scientist who studies plants, you'd call an aubergine a fruit, not a vegetable. But if you weren't a botanist, you'd probably call it a vegetable. Non-botanists just tend to use the word 'fruit' if something is sweet, and 'vegetable' if it isn't. So hardly anyone calls tomatoes fruit, even though they are. Sorry, botanists.

Fruity nuts

To add to the confusion, nuts are also classed as fruits. Unlike with most fruits though, where you eat the stuff that contains the seeds, with nuts, you eat the seed itself.

Toxic tomatoes

When tomatoes were first introduced to Europe and North America, people thought they were poisonous and didn't eat them – and they were right, sort of. Tomato plants do contain poison: an alkaloid called tomatine. Most of the tomatine is contained in the stem and leaves of the plant – so don't eat them – you could get very sick indeed. There is some poison in the fruit, but not enough to be dangerous. Tomatoes, potatoes, chillies and aubergines all come from the same family as a plant called 'deadly nightshade', which is very poisonous, as its name suggests.

Crazy aubergines

People in Europe also thought aubergines were poisonous, and might send anyone who ate them mad. The Italian word for aubergine, 'melanzane', means 'mad apple'. In China in the 5th century, women made a special dye from the skin of purple aubergines. They used it to stain and polish their teeth, so that they'd shine like metal – which was very fashionable at the time … believe it or not.

WHAT'S THE DIFFERENCE BETWEEN A TOWN AND A CITY?

Do you live in a town or a city? It's a question that's a lot more complicated than you might have thought.

Definitions of towns, cities and villages depend on all sorts of things: which country they're in, their history, and their size – though that last one isn't nearly as important as you might think. However, some parts of the world, such as France and Italy, just use one word for both.

If you live in the United Kingdom, you might live in a city that's actually smaller than a nearby town. In the past, a built-up urban area could be made a city because it had a cathedral – this was true in other parts of Europe, too – or because of royal connections. Today, city status can be granted because of size, history and importance – if a place has a university, for example. Preston in England and Newport in Wales both only became cities in the early 21st century. All this can mean that there are towns that are larger than some cities. Swindon in England is home to 155,000 people, but it's classed as a town, while St David's in Wales, which has a cathedral, is a city, even though only just over 1,700 people live there. St David's is Britain's smallest city.

In the United States, towns and cities are given their status under local state law. There aren't any nationwide rules about what qualifies as a city. In China, however, no one need be in any doubt about where they live: a city has to have at least 100,000 inhabitants who live and work in the urban area.

In Belgium, the Netherlands and Luxembourg, certain rights come with city status. For example: the right to charge tolls for travelling on some roads, put up city walls, or to mint official city coins. That might not sound very exciting, but the money from the tolls probably comes in handy – for building those walls perhaps – plus everyone living there gets to feel a bit superior. There's also an official list of cities, which are granted their status because of their history and importance but not necessarily because of their size. For example, the city of Staverden in the Netherlands has only 40 inhabitants, which is probably only about ten more people than there are in your class at school. Back in 1298, when it became a city, there was a hunting lodge for extremely posh people there – so it was exactly the kind of place the king thought was important enough to be a city, regardless of how many people lived there.

PACKED WITH PEOPLE

It's tricky to say for certain which are the most-populated cities in the world, but experts estimate that ...

... over **36 million** people live in **Tokyo**, Japan
... over **21 million** people live in **Delhi**, India
... over **19 million** people live in **Mumbai**, India
... over **19 million** people live in **Saõ Paulo**, Brazil
... over **19 million** people live in **Mexico City**, Mexico
... over **16 million** people live in **Shanghai**, China
... over **15 million** people live in **Kolkata**, India
... over **14 million** people live in **Dhaka**, Bangladesh
... over **13 million** people live in **Karachi**, Pakistan
... over **12 million** people live in **Beijing**, China.

Extreme cities

The world's most northerly city – of more than 100,000 people – is Norilsk in Russia. The world's most southerly city – of more than 100,000 people – is Punto Arenas in Chile.

Smallest country

The world's smallest country is Vatican City, where the Pope lives. It's tiny – less than half a square kilometre – and even though all of it lies inside the city of Rome in Italy, it's still a country in its own right. The population is around 800, but hardly anyone lives there permanently. It even has its own military force – the Swiss Guard, who are the Pope's bodyguards.

WHAT'S THE DIFFERENCE BETWEEN A MOUNTAIN AND A HILL?

Have you ever climbed up a slope so steep you thought you must be climbing more than just a hill? Just how big does a hill need to be before you can call it a mountain?

No one really knows the answer to this vital question because there's no official definition. At one time in the UK, a mountain was defined as an area of land standing over 1,000 feet – just over 600 metres – above the surrounding land. This definition was abandoned in the 1920s, quite possibly causing distressing uncertainty to hill-climbers all over the country. The United States adopted the same definition for a while too, but they also gave it up as a bad idea in the end.

A mountains or a hill can be defined in different ways by its height (obviously), steepness, and the general 'pointy-ness' of its summit. Some definitions state that a mountain must be over 1,200 metres tall, although there are several high-up places named as mountains that are significantly lower than this.

Unfortunately, no definition is agreed upon universally, so everyone will have to carry on uphill in confusion.

Sometimes, really enormous, steep things are known as hills, while relatively small bumps on the landscape are referred to as mountains. Here are a few of them.

Big hills

Tiger Hill in Darjeeling, India is absolutely massive by anybody's standards at 2,600 metres. But from it you can see the Himalayas – the tallest mountains in the world – so that's probably why it's just called a hill. Other enormous hills include the Black Hills of South Dakota at 2,200 metres and Cavanal Hill, Oklahoma, USA at 609 metres.

Small mountains

Some tiny mountains include: Mount Wycheproof, Australia, which stands at just 143 metres above sea level; Mollehoj, Denmark – the highest natural point in the country at 170 metres above sea level; and Mount Carmel, Israel at 525 metres above sea level.

Highest mountains

Mount Everest is the highest peak in the world, at 8,850 metres above sea level. But there are larger mountains on Earth … below the sea. Mauna Kea, one of the inactive volcanoes in the US state of Hawaii, measures 4,200 metres above sea level, but is actually 9,100 metres from its base on the sea floor.

Risky business

Hundreds of people have died trying to climb Mount Everest. It's an incredibly dangerous mountain to climb because of the extreme cold, which can lead to frostbite and hypothermia. Lack of oxygen can lead to altitude sickness (see below) and there's also the chance of plummeting to your death. That doesn't put people off – every year there are several expeditions to climb Mount Everest. Some people aren't content with one ascent: a man named Apa Sherpa had climbed Everest 21 times at the last count in 2011. And the youngest person ever to reach the summit was 13-year-old Jordan Romero, in 2010.

Travel sick

Acute Altitude Sickness is caused by the lower levels of oxygen at high altitudes. It occurs above 2,500 metres, and the most serious cases above 3,500. Sufferers feel exhausted and sick and get terrible headaches, and it can develop into a life-threatening condition. Low oxygen levels can also affect people's judgment – which is very tricky when you're halfway up a mountain!

WHAT'S THE DIFFERENCE BETWEEN A BISON AND A BUFFALO?

Both buffalo and bison are a bit like cows and both have horns – easy to confuse, but they are actually very different.

Bison have a shaggy coat in winter, which they shed in summer, while buffalo have a short, glossy coat. Their heads are shaped very differently, too: bison have a huge hump behind their heads, and buffalo don't. But buffalo win the prize for the biggest horns – some have horns as long as their bodies.

Both buffalo and bison are from the same family group, called 'Bovidae' in Latin. Cape buffalo, which are rather fierce (see next page), are native to Africa – water buffalo are native to Asia and are much more gentle. Bison are native to North America, where they were hunted by Native Americans and then – almost to extinction – by European settlers. There is also a European species of bison, known as wisents, which WERE hunted to extinction in the wild. Unfortunately for them, their impressive horns were popular as drinking horns in the Middle Ages. Though you'll be happy to know they've been reintroduced to the wild from captivity.

Bison in North America became known as American buffalo because the settlers thought they looked vaguely similar to their huge-horned cousins ... if you squinted a bit. The confusion lived on, and many people still believe that Native American hunters followed herds of buffalo, rather than bison, on the North American plains ... until you put them right.

Killer Cape buffalo

Never mess with a Cape buffalo ... they might look like big cows, but they're extremely aggressive and territorial. They can be huge – up to 3.5 metres long and nearly two metres tall, weighing up to a tonne. Their horns are sharp and deadly and, once they start to attack, they don't give up easily – imagine something the length and weight of a small car hurtling towards you – except taller and with horns. Cape buffalo are some of the most dangerous animals in Africa – they've even been known to kill lions!

Beefy bison

Bison are just as big as their cousins the Cape buffalo, though not as aggressive. There used to be tens of millions of bison in North America, but they were hunted so aggressively during the 19th century that bison numbers were reduced to a few hundred. Today there are around just 400,000 bison in North America.

WHAT'S THE DIFFERENCE BETWEEN A PLANET, A DWARF PLANET AND AN ASTEROID?

Poor Pluto, spinning away in the cold and dark, thousands of millions of miles away from the Sun. It used to be the ninth planet in the Solar System, but in 2006, it was demoted to a dwarf planet. Ever since, people have been scratching their heads about what makes a planet different from a dwarf planet, and what makes a dwarf planet different from an asteroid.

There are strict rules of admission to the Planet Club in the Solar System. A planet has to ...

● orbit the Sun.

● have a round, or nearly round, shape.

● have no other objects of a similar size in its orbit, other than its own satellites, or moons – things that are in orbit around the planet itself rather than the Sun.

Pluto orbits the Sun and it's nearly spherical, but sadly there are other objects in the same orbit – in an area of the Solar System beyond Neptune known as the Kuiper belt. At least Pluto is the biggest object in the Kuiper belt though.

29

Pint-sized planets

At the moment there are five 'dwarf planets' in the Solar System. In order of size, they are

ERIS. Eris orbits the Sun in the furthest reaches of the Solar System, part of what is called the 'scattered disc', made up of other icy asteroids. It's around 2,400 kilometres in diameter, which is roughly the distance between London, UK and Athens, Greece.

PLUTO. Pluto is part of the Kuiper belt. Around 2,300 kilometers in diameter.

MAKEMAKE. This is also part of the Kuiper belt. It's around 1,500 kilometres in diameter – a bit more than the distance between Land's End and John O' Groats – and is the most southwesterly and northeasterly places in the UK.

HAUMEA. Part of the Kuiper belt – it is roughly 1,150 kilometres in diameter.

CERES. Ceres is part of the asteroid belt – a collection of space debris, large and small, orbiting the Sun between Mars and Jupiter. It's about 975 kilometres in diameter.

All dwarf planets are asteroids, but only some asteroids can be called a dwarf planet. For example, an asteroid can't be called a dwarf planet if it's not spherical enough. If an object's gravity is strong enough, it's forced into a ball shape, because the gravity is pulling every bit of it towards the centre. But many asteroids look like lumpy potatoes, or misshapen sausages, or apples with huge chunks knocked out of them. Non-round asteroids are usually less than 400 kilometres in diameter – they aren't massive enough for their gravity to pull the surface of the asteroid inwards into a sphere shape.

MANY MOONS

Earth has only one moon. Venus and Mercury have none at all, but Jupiter has far more than its fair share: 62 at the last count. One of them, Ganymede, is the largest moon in the Solar System, and is bigger than the planet Mercury.

Scientists get excited about Titan, the largest of Saturn's moons, because it's the most likely place in the Solar System to support life, other than Earth. Titan is also bigger than Mercury.

Pluto may be only a dwarf planet these days, but it still has its own moon, Charon, which is more than half the size of Pluto itself. So at least it's got company.

Solar System survival guide

Ever wondered how you'd cope if you were suddenly transported to a distant part of the Solar System?

MERCURY is closest to the Sun, so it gets very hot during the day (430 °C) but very cold at night (-170 °C). But actually, being boiled or frozen is the least of your worries – the intense radiation from the Sun will kill you anyway.

VENUS is even hotter than Mercury because of its atmosphere, which is mostly carbon dioxide. You'd be roasted, squished by the massive pressure of the atmosphere, and sizzled by clouds of poisonous sulphuric acid.

MARS has an atmosphere that is mostly carbon dioxide, too, so you wouldn't be able to breathe – but apart from that it wouldn't be too bad.

Don't even think about visiting a gas giant though (JUPITER, SATURN, URANUS OR NEPTUNE), unless you can fly through poisonous gas, or swim through liquid methane. They're also absolutely freezing, ridiculously windy – winds on Neptune blow at 2,000 kilometres per hour – and prone to violent storms. One storm on Jupiter has been raging for the last 300 years.

WHAT'S THE DIFFERENCE BETWEEN A LLAMA AND AN ALPACA?

They're both from South America, and they both look like enormous sheep with long necks ... so what's the difference?

Both llamas and alpacas are part of the same family group as camels – the Latin name is 'Camelidae'. The two animals share a common wild ancestor, but people have bred them over thousands of years for different purposes. The llama has been bred to be big and strong, so that it can carry things, while the alpaca has been bred to produce lovely soft wool. They do look similar, but in fact there are a lot of differences between the two animals.

Llamas are much larger and stronger – they're roughly twice the size of an alpaca.

Llamas have a double coat, with a coarse outer layer and a softer inner layer. It can be spun into wool.

Alpacas have a soft, single coat that makes fine wool. You can get much more wool from an alpaca than from a llama, even though alpacas are so much smaller.

Llamas have straighter backs and straighter ears.

'INCA-REDIBLE' ANIMALS

GUANACOS and VICUNAS are wild South American animals very similar to llamas and alpacas. Vicunas are thought to be the wild ancestor of alpacas: they also produce fine wool, though not very much of it and they can only be shorn every three years. The Inca people, who once ruled a big chunk of South America, prized vicuna wool very highly. It was so valuable to them that only the Incan emperor and his family were allowed to wear it.

The huarizo is the MULE (see page 54) of the llama world. It is the result of a male llama breeding with a female alpaca. A huarizo fleece makes good wool like an alpaca's does, but there's a lot more of it because huarizos are bigger.

LLAMAS were very important to the native people of South America because there were no horses around to carry things. The Incas were said to be terrified when they first saw Spanish invaders riding horses - they'd never seen people riding animals before.

WHAT'S THE DIFFERENCE BETWEEN A COLD AND THE FLU?

The flu is just like a cold – except it sounds worse, so it's a better excuse for a day off. Right? Er, no.

Colds and flu, which is short for influenza, are both caused by illnesses known as viruses (see page 59), but different ones. Colds are caused by a wide variety of different viruses, while flu is caused by specific influenza viruses – types A, B or C. Type A is generally the most serious. All these viruses are spread by tiny droplets in the air or by hand contact … you might want to go and wash your hands at this point.

A bad cold might make you spend time in bed feeling terrible, but it won't kill you and it's usually gone after a week or so. Flu can be more serious – it can make you feel much worse than a cold, it has different symptoms, and it can kill people in high-risk groups, such as the very young, the very old, or people who have lung or heart diseases. Sometimes, though very rarely, it can kill perfectly healthy, young people, too.

If you're still not sure whether you have a cold or the flu, check your symptoms:

COLDS:
• give you a runny nose, swollen sinuses (at the top of your nose) and make you sneeze a lot.
• might make you a bit hot and feverish.
• might give you aches and pains and a bit of a headache.

FLU:
• often causes a sore throat, but no runny nose or sneezing.
• makes you very hot and feverish.
• usually gives you a terrible headache and aches and pains all over your body.
• might also give you chills, make you feel weak and sick and stop you feeling hungry.

You can catch a cold at any time of year, but they're more common in the winter because central heating dries out the snot in your nose that helps keep viruses at bay.

The best way to avoid colds and flu is to wash your hands regularly. There are flu vaccines available, recommended for older people or people with specific illnesses. However, they're not always effective because viruses can change so that they aren't affected by the vaccine.

Fatal Flu

The worst outbreak of flu was the Spanish Flu of 1918-1919, which killed between 30 and 50 million people all over the world. The First World War had just ended, but even more people died from the flu than had died in the war.

WHAT'S THE DIFFERENCE BETWEEN A MUSHROOM AND A TOADSTOOL?

Is a mushroom edible and a toadstool poisonous? Or are toadstools the red ones with white dots that gnomes sit on?

In fact, there isn't really a difference between toadstools and mushrooms at all. They're both types of fungus. A fungus isn't a plant or an anima: – like plants, animals, algae and bacteria, it has its own 'kingdom', which is a category of living things. There are more than 1.5 million species in the fungus kingdom, which includes tiny organisms such as moulds and yeasts, as well as mushrooms. Surprisingly, and rather spookily, studies have shown that fungus is more closely related to animals than to plants.

A fungus that you can eat is often called a mushroom, whereas one you can't is often called a toadstool. Although people might call an inedible fungus a mushroom, they wouldn't call an edible one a toadstool. But there's no scientific definition of either word.

The red funguses (or fungi) with white spots on, which you might think of as typical toadstools, are 'Amanita muscaria', commonly known as 'fly agaric'. They are poisonous, though not as deadly as some other types of fungus. Scientists are still debating whether these are the toadstools preferred by gnomes.

Poisonous funguses aren't necessarily the most brightly coloured – some of the most deadly are a harmless-looking whitish colour. If you don't want to risk dying an agonizing death, never eat a mushroom or toadstool unless it's been identified as edible by an expert. Or, preferably, several experts, who have all eaten some first.

● ●

FUNGUS FACTS

Some forms of fungus can be helpful to humans, but others can be very bad indeed. Yeasts, which are a type of fungus, make bread rise and ferment beer. Funguses are used to manufacture medicines and detergents, and there are even ones that glow in the dark. However, on the down side, fungal diseases can destroy crops, and many types of fungus produce toxins that are lethal to humans and other animals.

● ●

Deadly death cap

The death cap, or 'Amanita phalloides', is responsible for the most deaths by mushroom poisoning. After three days of vomiting, diarrhoea and dizziness, you begin to feel better – but in fact your liver is being destroyed, and you're usually dead in a couple more days.

Murderous mushrooms

Don't be fooled by thinking that anything poisonous must taste bad. Poisonous mushrooms can be tasty. It's thought that the Roman Emperor Claudius was murdered when he was given a dish of his favourite mushrooms to eat. Unfortunately another, deadly variety was also on the plate, and he ate the lot.

WHAT'S THE DIFFERENCE BETWEEN GOTHS, VISIGOTHS AND OSTROGOTHS?

This has nothing to do with people who dress in black and wear a lot of white make-up and black eyeliner. Unlike modern-day goths, who first appeared in the 1980s, the Goths were a barbarian tribe who lived in what is now Scandinavia and eastern Europe. In the 5th and 6th centuries, the Goths split into two separate tribes: the Ostrogoths and the Visigoths. The Ostrogoths, or eastern Goths, eventually ruled over most of Italy, after the fall of the Roman Empire. The Romans were bothered by various barbarians, including both types of Goth, until eventually the barbarians took over their empire completely.

SO, WHAT YOU'RE SAYING IS THAT THERE'S NO REAL DIFFERENCE BETWEEN US GOTHS, OSTROGOTHS AND VISIGOTHS?

The Visigoths, or western Goths, had their kingdom in what's now part of southern France. Another tribe, the Franks, pushed them out of France and further west to Spain, where they were eventually defeated by the Moors – invaders from North Africa.

Some other barbarian tribes

HUNS: most famous for being the scariest barbarians of all. They conquered a huge empire under their terrifying leader, Attila the Hun.

FRANKS: most famous for conquering the whole of Gaul – once the Frankish tribes were united, which is why Gaul is called France today.

VANDALS: most famous for laying waste to Rome in AD 455. Modern-day vandals are named after them.

THE FALL OF THE ROMAN EMPIRE
(AND A BARBARIAN)

The Roman Empire gradually declined, partly due to the rampaging barbarians. It split into two - the western empire, ruled from Rome, and the eastern, or Byzantine, empire, ruled from Constantinople - modern-day Istanbul. In AD 476, the barbarian Odoacer kicked the last emperor of the western empire out of Rome and became King of Italy, ending the Roman Empire, at least in the west, once and for all.

Attila the Hun, fearsome warrior and king, and general of the Huns for 20 years, survived bloody battles against the Roman Army but died from a nosebleed. Apparently, he drank too much on his wedding night, passed out, had a nosebleed and choked on his own blood.

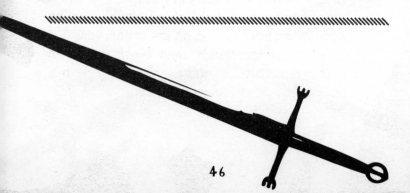

WHAT'S THE DIFFERENCE BETWEEN A WHITE RHINO AND A BLACK RHINO?

This should be obvious, but in fact both types of rhino are grey, both live in Africa, they look very similar, and have two horns. White rhinos are called that, not because they're white – they're grey, as you know – but because Dutch settlers in Africa described them as 'wijd'. It was translated into English as 'white', but really means 'wide'. The settlers were thought to be referring to the rhinos' mouths. Black rhinos are called black rhinos ... because white rhinos are called white rhinos. Neither name has anything to do with skin colour.

There are differences between these two African rhinoceroses that don't have to do with colour though. Here are a few:

WHITE RHINOS ...

... have a wide, square upper lip.
... are likely to be seen in groups.
... are larger than black rhinos - they're about the same size as an ice-cream van.
... have larger heads than black rhinos in proportion to their body - they also have a sort of hump behind their heads.

BLACK RHINOS ...

... have a hooked upper lip, a bit like a beak.
... prefer to live on their own.
... are smaller than white rhinos.
... have smaller heads than white rhinos in proportion to their body. Although they're smaller, black rhinos are more aggressive than white rhinos, so watch out!

Other rhinos

White and black rhinos are the two African rhino species. There are three others:

The Indian rhinoceros, or the Greater One-horned Rhinoceros, is about the same size as a white rhino, but has one horn. Its great folds of thick skin make it look armour-plated. It lives in Nepal and northeastern India.

48

The Javan rhinoceros also has one horn, and similar armour-plated-looking skin to the Indian rhino, though it's a bit smaller. The species is critically endangered and is only found in two national parks – one in Java, Indonesia, and the other in Vietnam.

The Sumatran rhinoceros is the smallest of the rhinos, and also the most hairy. It's also critically endangered and is found in Sumatra, Borneo and Malaysia.

HORN TODAY, GONE TOMORROW

All rhinos are endangered. This is partly because the areas where they live are becoming smaller, as towns and cities grow into the surrounding countryside. Rhinos are sometimes killed for their horns, too, which are supposed to have medicinal properties, and are also used to make traditional dagger handles in the Middle East.

WHAT'S THE DIFFERENCE BETWEEN POETRY AND PROSE?

Surely the difference is obvious ... isn't it? You won't find rhyming in prose – that's the kind of writing you find in stories or, well, books like this. But of course not all poems rhyme. For example ...

Roses are red
Violets are blue
Some poems rhyme
But this one doesn't

So that doesn't help very much.

Prose is written in sentences and paragraphs, but poetry is written in lines, which are sometimes separated into verses, or stanzas. However, not all poetry is written down – the first poems were recited, and people learned them by heart and passed them on. The Iliad – an ancient Greek poem about the Trojan War, which was fought between the Greeks and the Trojans – is an example of this. So even when a poem isn't written down, it's still a poem. And before the Middle Ages, poems were often written down without breaks between the lines. So even when a poem isn't written down in lines and stanzas, it's still a poem.

Perhaps the best thing to say that poetry has a pattern – a metrical structure, or rhythm, and sometimes a rhyming structure – that prose doesn't.

The world's first ... accounts

The first written words we know about were written by the Sumerian people of Mesopotamia — modern-day Iraq — around 5,500 years ago. The subject wasn't very exciting: just records and accounts. The ancient Sumerians used reeds to make marks on clay, which is how the writing has survived — if they had used paper it would have rotted away.

Really old poems

The oldest poem to be written down — as far as anyone knows — also comes from ancient Sumer. It's called the Epic of Gilgamesh and was written around 4,000 years ago. It's about King Gilgamesh, who was probably a real king around 2,500 BC. The Iliad and the Odyssey are ancient Greek poems, which were written around 700 BC — though they'd been spoken aloud for a long time before that. The Iliad is about the Trojan War, and the Odyssey is about Odysseus, a Greek warrior, and his long journey home from the Trojan War. The word 'odyssey' entered the English language and means a long, difficult journey.

Really, really long poems

The Iliad, the Odyssey and Gilgamesh are all long poems – in those days, apparently, a couple of verses just wasn't enough. But the world's longest poem is the Mahabharata, an Indian poem written in the ancient language Sanskrit. It's about four times the length of the Iliad and Odyssey combined – around 100,000 verses, and 1.8 million words. It would take several days to recite it, without pausing to eat or sleep.

WHAT'S THE DIFFERENCE BETWEEN ASSES, MULES AND DONKEYS?

At last, an end to your mule confusion ... the difference between an ass and a donkey is easy to explain: there isn't one. 'Ass' is just another name for a donkey.

Donkeys are members of the horse family, called 'Equidae' in Latin, so you could say that donkeys are horses, too. Like horses, donkeys have been kept by humans for thousands of years, but they're descended from wild donkeys, such as the African Wild Ass.

A mule is the result of a female horse mating with a male donkey. The result of a male horse mating with a female donkey, which is much more rare, is called a hinny. Usually, mules and hinnies can't breed – so at least the confusion stops there.

Jacks and jennies

A male donkey is known as a 'jack' and a female is known as a 'jenny'.

Zebra Crossings

Zebras are also part of the horse family group and they can also breed with donkeys. You might not have heard of zebroids, zedonks and zebrasses, but they do exist. They're the offspring of a female donkey and a male zebra. If a male donkey and a female zebra produce offspring, it's called a zebra hinny, or a zebrinny, though this is much rarer.

Zebra Stripes

Zebras' distinctive stripes make them easy to spot – it's almost as if they wanted to draw attention to themselves, the show-offs. But zebras wouldn't stand out so much if you were a lion, because lions can't tell the difference between colours in the same way that humans can. The stripes help to confuse lions and other predators because they make it tricky for them to pick out an individual animal, which is how lions usually hunt. Zebras might all look alike to you, and to lions, too, but in fact each zebra's stripe pattern is unique, like a person's fingerprint.

Giant Donkeys

Donkeys are generally smaller than horses – the smallest are less than a metre tall when measured to their shoulders. But there's one breed of wild donkey in southern Spain that reaches 1.5 metres – as big as a race horse.

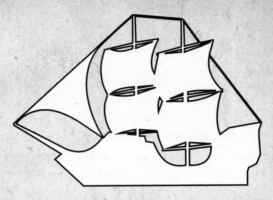

WHAT'S THE DIFFERENCE BETWEEN A SHIP AND A BOAT?

Are you wondering about the correct word to describe your luxury ocean-going yacht?

Ships are large. They are designed for crossing seas rather than staying near the coast, or sailing on rivers and lakes like boats. 'Large' isn't very precise, but there's no official size at which a boat becomes a ship.

Before the days of motorized vessels, a ship had to have at least three masts with square-rigged sails. But that seems a bit old-fashioned today, now that we no longer rely on wind power to move boats and ships around.

There's a simple, though unofficial, way of telling the difference between ships and boats: a ship must be big enough to carry boats, and a boat must be small enough to be carried by a ship. But a submarine is always called a boat, no matter how big it is.

If you're still wondering about your yacht, it's best just to call it a yacht, which sounds more posh anyway, unless it's under 12 metres long, in which case it's a mere cabin cruiser.

A USELESS GIANT

The Seawise Giant - first renamed the Happy Giant, Jahre Viking, Knock Nevis, and finally Mont - was the longest and heaviest ship ever built. If you stood it on its end, it would have been taller than the Empire State Building. Its last voyage was made in 2010 to India, for demolition. It was so big, it couldn't dock at many of the world's major ports, and couldn't navigate the Suez and Panama Canals or the English Channel. So it was impressive, but a bit pointless.

WHAT'S THE DIFFERENCE BETWEEN GERMS, VIRUSES AND BACTERIA?

Exactly what kinds of horrors are lurking on door handles and toilet seats? It's time they were identified ...

A germ is an informal word that means any microscopic organism that can cause disease. So viruses and bacteria are both 'germs'.

Viruses are really tiny and very simple - they can only be seen with a powerful electron microscope. Viruses can't grow or reproduce on their own - they have to infect living cells, taking them over and turning them into virus-producing factories. It sounds like an especially nasty horror story, but it happens billions of times a day, and could even be happening right now inside your own body. Aaargh!

There are millions of different viruses, and different kinds infect plants, animals, and even bacteria. In humans, viruses cause colds and flu (see page 37) and much more serious conditions such as the deadly diseases ebola and AIDS.

Bacteria are bigger than viruses, but you'd still need a microscope to see one. They're single-celled living organisms and they are able to reproduce. In fact, bacteria live just about everywhere on Earth, even in the most inhospitable conditions (see, for example, snottites on page 152, which live in hot, acidic sulphur caves). Most bacteria are not harmful to humans and many are beneficial – for example, bacteria that live in your intestines help with your digestion.

There are some bacteria that cause infections in people – some of them life-threatening. Not so long ago, bacterial infections were very dangerous – people often died from them. Luckily for us, in the middle of the 20th century, the first antibiotic – penicillin – was discovered by Alexander Fleming, a scientist with a messy laboratory who found bacteria-killing mould on a petri dish. From then on, bacterial infections began to be treated with antibiotics and far fewer people have died as a result. Phew.

SNEEZE ON THE MOON

In 1967 a Moon lander was sent up to the Moon to take pictures. Three years later, when it was brought back, some bacteria was found on the camera lens - it had survived being sent into space, extremes of temperature (-200 $^{\circ}$C to 200 $^{\circ}$C) and no atmosphere. It was traced back to a NASA technician who had sneezed in the lab where the equipment was tested.

ANCIENT BACTERIA

The oldest living thing ever found on Earth was bacteria. It was found in a state of suspended animation - a bit like hibernation - in sea-salt, then reanimated in a lab. It was 250 million years old, so it was around at the same time as the very first dinosaurs.

SMELLY BACTERIA

Bacteria smells - anyone who's ever owned a pair of trainers knows that. But scientists have discovered that bacteria has a very basic sense of smell, too - a 2010 experiment showed that bacteria can detect the smelly gas ammonia, and respond to it by producing a 'biofilm' or slime.

They both have enormous jaws and very sharp teeth, so you might not want to get close enough to find out ...

Both crocodiles and alligators belong to the same reptile family group, called 'Crocodylia'. So, as with frogs and toads on pages 11 to 12, all alligators are really crocodiles, but not all crocodiles are alligators.

There are 23 species in the crocodile family, divided into three smaller groups. Alligators are in one group, and crocodiles are in another. The third group has only one lonely member, the gharial, which has a really long snout. Male gharials have a round bump on the end of their snouts, just to show off.

MEMBERS OF THE ALLIGATOR FAMILY ...

... have U-shaped snouts, which are stronger than crocodiles' snouts and enable them to crack open turtle shells.

... are native only to North, South and Central America and China.

... live mostly in fresh water.

... have wider upper jaws than lower jaws, so you can see their upper teeth when their mouths are closed, but not their lower ones.

MEMBERS OF THE CROCODILE FAMILY ...

... have V-shaped snouts.

... can live in salt water as well as fresh water because they have special salt glands.

... have visible upper and lower teeth when their mouths are closed.

The easiest way to tell the creatures apart is to look at the shape of their jaws, but do keep your distance while you're doing it. Of course, there are exceptions to the general rules – for example, the Indian mugger crocodile has jaws which look very like an alligator's. If your Crocodylian does have a V-shaped snout, beware: crocodiles tend to be more aggressive towards humans than alligators.

Big and small

The world's largest crocodiles are saltwater crocodiles, which can grow to more than six metres long (if its head was touching one football goalpost, its tail would almost reach across to the other). The largest alligator ever, measured in Florida, was more than five metres long. The smallest member of either family is the West African dwarf crocodile, which grows to a maximum of 1.9 metres – and that's probably still longer than your dad is tall.

Old crocs

The ancestors of alligators and crocodiles were alive at the time of the dinosaurs – they've been on Earth for 240 million years.

WHAT'S THE DIFFERENCE BETWEEN A PTERODACTYL, A PTEROSAUR AND A PTERANODON?

Are scientists out to confuse everyone with lots of different words for the same thing?

You've probably heard people talking about 'pterodactyls', but there's really no such thing. A 'pterodactylus' was a type of small flying reptile that lived in the time of the dinosaurs, during the Jurassic period – about 200 million years ago. It was a type of pterosaur, which is the name for the family of flying reptiles that includes lots of others, such as pteranodons.

Pterodactylus was the first pterosaur ever to be discovered, in 1784. That might be why a shortened form of the word, 'pterodactyl', is often used to mean any prehistoric flying lizard. The correct term for this is pterosaur, as you can now point out. Pteranodons were a group of pterosaurs quite different from their smaller cousins, pterodactylus. Here are some of the differences between them:

Pterodactylus ...

... had teeth.
... was quite small — the smallest were only around the length of a ruler, and even the biggest had a wingspan of under a metre.
... had no head crest.

Pteranodon ...

... was toothless.
... was much bigger — the biggest had wingspans of about nine metres.
... had a huge backwards-facing head crest.

PTEROSAUR TRIVIA

The largest pterosaur wasn't the pteranodon but the Quetzalcoatlus, which had a wingspan of about 12 metres - about the length of a bus.

Modern birds aren't descended from pterosaurs, which didn't have feathers, but from two-legged, meat-eating dinosaurs.

Pterodactylus and pteranodons are often called dinosaurs but they're not. Dinosaurs were land animals. So all the sea creatures from the time of the dinosaurs, such as plesiosaurs and ichthyosaurs, aren't dinosaurs either.

I MAY BE SMALL BUT I BET I COULD GIVE YOU A NASTY BITE!

WHAT'S THE DIFFERENCE BETWEEN PETROL AND DIESEL?

Both make cars go, but why is it so important not to fill a petrol car with diesel, or a diesel car with petrol?

Petrol and diesel are both made from crude oil, which occurs naturally beneath the Earth's surface. Crude oil can be refined to make other kinds of fuel, too, such as kerosene, which is used in some portable stoves and heaters and is also called paraffin. Most cars run on either petrol or diesel.

Diesel, or diesel oil, is much thicker and oilier than petrol. And it's not nearly as flammable – if you dropped a lighted match into some petrol it would erupt into flames instantly, but if you dropped a match into diesel it wouldn't even catch fire. (Do NOT try this at home, just in case.)

Petrol engines and diesel engines both convert fuel into energy that drives a vehicle's wheels around, and gets you to the cinema or shops or school. Both engines make the fuel into energy by creating a series of explosions. Since petrol catches fire easily, petrol engines use electrical devices called spark plugs to cause a small spark and set fire to the petrol. Diesel engines compress air, which makes it extremely hot, and makes the diesel catch fire when it is added.

If you're wondering which fuel is better for the environment …

• **A litre of diesel has more energy in it than a litre of petrol, so diesel cars can drive further for each litre of fuel used.**

• **Petrol engines create carbon monoxide, carbon dioxide and other compounds that are bad for the environment and for people, which are pumped into the air through exhaust pipes.**

• **Diesel cars' exhaust fumes contain tiny particles of soot and poisonous nitrogen compounds, which are very bad for people's lungs.**

In other words, they're both pretty bad. The world's oil is going to run out eventually, so we need to come up with an alternative – or start cycling a lot more. What we really need is a cheap, efficient fuel that has no nasty waste products. Maybe in the future we'll all be getting about using personal jet packs powered by vegetable oil – perhaps you could invent a new fuel, and save the planet in the process? The rest of us would be very grateful.

THE CARS OF THE FUTURE

Millions of pounds are being spent on research into cars that run on electricity, hydrogen and compressed air. The 'greenest', most environmentally friendly, cars available today combine a petrol engine with an electric motor, which pump far fewer nasty chemicals into the air than petrol-only or diesel-only cars do.

WHAT'S THE DIFFERENCE BETWEEN TANGERINES, SATSUMAS AND CLEMENTINES?

What's really in your fruit bowl? If it's a small version of an orange, slightly flat on each end and with looser skin, then it's a mandarin orange. Tangerines, satsumas and clementines are all varieties of mandarin. If you had one of each in front of you, you'd probably need to be an expert to tell the difference. But here are some hints to help you ...

Tangerines have seeds – they tend to be smaller than satsumas.

Satsumas tend to be larger than tangerines, with yellower skin. They don't have seeds – at least, most of them don't.

Clementines are seedless too – with some exceptions. They're likely to have a more orange-coloured skin than a satsuma.

Smelly fruit

If you go to Southeast Asia you might be offered a spiky fruit called a 'durian'. Think twice before you accept: its smell is absolutely awful, described as similar to old socks, turpentine, or even sewage. Some people don't mind the smell, and lots of people like the taste of the fruit, even those who find the smell revolting. The smell is so strong that the fruit is banned on public transport and from some hotels in Southeast Asia.

Lucky fruit

In China, mandarin oranges are considered to be lucky. At Chinese New Year they're given as good luck gifts.

WHAT'S THE DIFFERENCE BETWEEN A MONKEY AND AN APE?

If you ever meet a large male gorilla, the last thing you want to do is offend him by not knowing whether he's a monkey or an ape. After all, you're very closely related. And he's at least ten times stronger than you are.

Monkeys and apes both belong to the same group of animals, known as primates. People, lemurs – a monkey-like creature with big eyes and a long tail, and tarsiers – a monkey-like animal with even bigger eyes, which looks a bit like a bushbaby, are also primates. All primates have forward-facing eyes and quite large brains – some much larger than others.

Apes include gorillas, chimpanzees, orang-utans, gibbons and people, while monkeys are just about everything else (except lemurs and tarsiers). There are different kinds of gibbon, which are all collectively known as the 'lesser apes'. The other types of ape are known as 'great apes'.

The most obvious difference between apes and monkeys is that apes don't have tails. Most monkeys do – but not all of them. Here are some more differences:

Monkeys can't swing from branch to branch as apes – and humans – can because of their bone structure. They run along branches instead.

Monkeys tend to spend more of their time in trees than apes do. They use their tails as a fifth limb – useful for climbing trees and hanging around in them.

Apes are generally bigger than monkeys. Except gibbons, which are smaller than some monkeys.

Most apes have arms longer than their legs, while monkeys' arms are the same length as their legs or shorter.

OUR COUSINS, THE CHIMPS

We share much of our genetic make-up with gorillas, but chimpanzees are our closest living relatives. Millions of years ago, chimps and humans had a common ancestor. Just like humans, chimps use tools: they use stones as hammers to crack open nuts, and use straw and sticks to dig out termites to eat. They also plan and cooperate with one another to hunt. In captivity, chimps have been taught to communicate with humans using sign language.

WHAT'S THE DIFFERENCE BETWEEN THE NETHERLANDS AND HOLLAND?

In English, 'the Netherlands' and 'Holland' are both used to refer to the same country, and not many people seem to bother with which word they use. There's similar confusion in lots of other languages, too. But really they mean different things.

North Holland and South Holland are both regions of the Netherlands. There are ten other regions within the Netherlands, including Gelderland, Friesland, Zeeland and Utrecht. In the past, Holland was the most powerful region in the Netherlands, and sometimes even Dutch people say Holland when they're talking about the whole country of the Netherlands. It's a bit like saying 'England' when referring to the whole of the United Kingdom, and some people get upset about it. The correct term is the Netherlands, so, to be sure you're not annoying a Dutch person from Friesland, always use the Netherlands instead of Holland.

There's an exception, though: the Netherlands' national football team is known as Holland, at least outside of the Netherlands, because it's the best-known word in other countries. The team has Holland on its shirts, even though it's the national team. It's the same for some other sports teams from the Netherlands, too.

Luckily there's no such confusion about the language and people of the Netherlands: they're both Dutch.

NETHER NETHERLAND

Netherlands means 'lowlands', and the country is very low indeed – 20% of it is below sea level, and half of it is only a metre above sea level. The sea is kept out with clever engineering – the Dutch use strong, high walls called dikes to keep out the sea and reclaim land, and canals to collect water and pump it back into the sea.

WHAT'S THE DIFFERENCE BETWEEN INFECTIOUS AND CONTAGIOUS?

You've just broken out in green spots. But are you infectious or contagious?

An infection is a disease caused by a microscopic germ, which could be bacteria or a virus (see page 59). A cold is an infectious disease, so is chicken pox, so is athlete's foot, and so is malaria – the deadly disease that's spread by the bite of a mosquito. There are thousands of them ... but try not to worry too much!

A disease is contagious when it's capable of being spread directly from person to person. This can happen by touch, or when you share someone's drinking straw, or – in the case of athlete's foot – step into the shower after someone else. If someone with a cold sneezes, tiny droplets in the air can find their way into another person's body and pass on the disease that way.

There are lots of diseases, such as colds and flu, that are infectious and contagious. In fact, if a disease is contagious, it must also be infectious, because only diseases caused by germs can be passed from person to person. But not all infectious diseases are contagious: malaria, for example, can't be spread from person to person – you can only get it from a mosquito bite.

There are also many diseases, such as cancer and heart disease, that aren't caused by an infection, and so can't be passed from person to person. They're neither infectious nor contagious.

It's up to you to work out how you got the green spots.

● ● ● ● ● ● ● ● ● ● ● ● ● ● ● ● ●

DEADLY DISEASES

The disease responsible for the most deaths every year is heart disease, which isn't infectious or contagious. But around one in eight deaths is caused by an infectious disease, such as malaria, tuberculosis, AIDS, cholera or dysentery.

Measles is passed more easily from person to person than any other disease, making it the most contagious in the world. You were probably given an injection when you were small to stop you getting it, but lots of people around the world aren't injected, and hundreds of thousands of children die from measles every year.

● ● ● ● ● ● ● ● ● ● ● ● ● ● ●

81

WHAT'S THE DIFFERENCE BETWEEN A WEASEL AND A STOAT?

A weasel is 'weasily' recognized — a stoat is 'stoatally' different — right?

Well, not really. Weasels and stoats are both members of the same family group, and they're both very similar. They're both small, sleek carnivorous mammals that prey on mice and other, smaller mammals, and sometimes birds and eggs. And they're both light brown with a pale underside. In fact, unless you can persuade them to sit on a set of scales, it's tricky to tell the difference.

Stoats are often a bit longer than weasels — weasels can be up to 25 centimetres, stoats up to about 30 centimetres — and they're usually much bigger. Stoats can weigh up to 450 grams — more than most cats, while weasels weigh up to 120 grams. Unlike weasels, stoats have a black tip to their tail, and usually change their coats in winter, when they become white — though they still keep their black tail tips.

Ferrets

Ferrets are members of the same family as weasels and stoats, and they're descended from wild polecats. They've been kept by humans for thousands of years — originally to hunt rabbits. Nowadays, they're popular pets.

'FURRY' EXPENSIVE

Stoats are also known as ermines, prized for the fur of their white winter coats. In the past, ermine was used to trim the grand outfits of kings and queens and other VIPs: it was so expensive that only the very rich could afford it. Lots of stoat skins would be used to make a single piece of clothing, with the black tails forming a regular pattern.

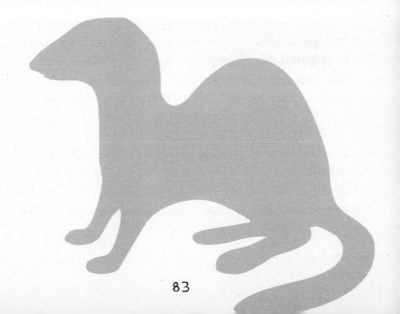

WHAT'S THE DIFFERENCE BETWEEN A HERB AND A SPICE?

The words herb and spice both mean the edible part of a plant used to flavour food. So is there actually a difference between them? Do we really need two words, or can we just pick our favourite and use that?

In the United States, people often choose whichever word they feel like using all the time. But generally:

HERBS are the leafy parts of a plant used for flavouring food. They come from countries that have fairly mild winters and summers that aren't too hot, like the UK. They can be used dried or fresh. For example: parsley, basil and thyme.

SPICES can be a plant's seeds, root, bark or berries. They tend to come from tropical countries. They can also be used dried or fresh, too, and they're often stronger in flavour than herbs. For example: cinnamon, cumin and pepper.

Some herbs can also be spices (and the other way around). Coriander, for example, can be both a herb and a spice – the leaves can be used to flavour food, and so can the seeds, which can be dried and ground. Dill seeds can be used as a spice, and its leaves can be used as a herb.

Which bit?
It's not always clear which bit of a plant a spice comes from:

Saffron – stamen of a crocus flower

Ginger – root

Vanilla – seed pod of an orchid

Cinnamon – bark of a tree

Cumin – seed

Paprika – dried fruit (peppers or chillies)

Popular pepper
Pepper is the world's most popular spice. It's not very expensive now, but during the time of the Roman Empire it was so valuable that it was known as 'black gold' and sometimes used as currency.

Hot and spicy
In ancient times, cinnamon was burned on funeral pyres to mask the smell of the burning body. The Roman Emperor Nero is said to have burned a whole year's supply of cinnamon at his wife's funeral to show that there was no expense spared for his dear wife – even though, in fact, he'd murdered her.

WHAT'S THE DIFFERENCE BETWEEN A HORSE AND A PONY?

It turns out that this a bit more confusing than you might have thought ...

The most obvious difference between a horse and a pony is size and, inconveniently for us, horses and ponies have a whole system of measurement all to themselves. In the UK, Australia and the US, horses and ponies are measured in 'hands'. One hand was originally the width of a man's hand, but because not all people has the same sized hands, everyone has now agreed that a hand should be four inches, which is just over 10 centimetres. If someone tells you their horse is 'fifteen two', that means it measures fifteen hands and two inches. Or, if you want to move into the 21st century, about 155 centimetres. A horse is always measured to the height of its 'withers', or shoulder blades, so its head is higher than its official height.

Using this old-fashioned system of measurement, for a pony to be described as a horse it must be 14.2 hands or over. The International Federation for Equestrian Sports, which uses metric, puts the height requirement at 148 centimetres without shoes, or 149 centimetres with them), which is just over 14.2 hands. So that's all pretty clear …

… unless you're in Australia, where a horse is a horse if it's over 14 hands. In fact, the Australians have an extra category – horses between 14 and 15 hands high are known as 'galloways'.

However, some breeds are always considered ponies or horses even if the animals are over or under the height rule. For example:

• **The Falabella is 76 centimetres, or 7.2 hands, at most – quite a bit smaller than a Great Dane dog, but still classified as a miniature horse.**

• **Icelandic horses are usually less than 14 hands.**

• **Arabian horses are often a bit shorter than 14.2 hands.**

Ponies are also usually stockier, stronger and more resistant to cold weather than horses. And more intelligent, too.

Horse words

If the closest you've ever been to a horse is playing with your little sister's My Little Pony, you can still go down to your local stable and sound like you know what you're talking about. The words opposite can be used to describe zebras and asses, as well as horses and ponies.

MARE: a female horse or pony.

STALLION: a male horse or pony.

FOAL: a horse or pony under a year old.

FILLY: a female foal, horse or pony under four years.

COLT: a male foal, horse or pony under four years.

YEARLING: a horse or pony between one and two years old.

Big and small

The largest horse on record was a shire horse called Mammoth, born in 1848. He was 21.2 ½ hands high, or 220 centimetres – probably taller than the top of a door in your house, and that was only to his shoulder. The smallest horse is Thumbelina, born in 2001. A miniature horse affected by dwarfism, she is 43 centimetres tall – shorter than a Labrador dog!

Old nags

Most domestic horses live to around 25 years old. But Old Billy, the oldest horse on record, lived for 62 years. He pulled barges along canals in the 18th and early 19th centuries. More recently, a pony called Sugar Puff died in 2007 aged 56.

WHAT'S THE DIFFERENCE BETWEEN LICE AND FLEAS?

Lice and fleas are both wingless, blood-sucking parasites (no offence). They're both insects – six-legged creatures with a skeleton on the outside of their three-sectioned bodies. Since they suck blood – and various types can live on humans – both are best avoided.

They might be horrible in very similar ways, but lice and fleas come from completely different groups of creatures. Here are some of the differences between them:

FLEAS ...

... get around by jumping – they can jump many times their own height.
... move around a lot.
... live by sucking blood.

LICE ...

... crawl around – they can't jump.
... don't move around much. They're likely to spend their entire lives on one animal.
... don't all suck blood. Some scavenge, and can be useful to the animals they live on – by keeping them clean, for example.

Three different types of lice live on humans. The most common are headlice.

Ticks and mites

Ticks and mites are also bloodsucking parasites, but they're not insects – they have eight legs, like spiders. They can carry serious diseases, such as Lyme disease, which people can get from deer ticks.

Historic lice

Lice have been useful to the study of history. Human body lice evolved from headlice around 170,000 years ago. Because body lice lay eggs and live most of the time in human clothing, it's very unlikely that the lice would have evolved without people wearing clothes for them to live in. So we know that people began to wear clothes around 170,000 years ago.

High jump

The champion jumper of the flea world is the cat flea, which can jump 20 centimetres high – 80 times the length of its own body. Champion human high jumpers can only manage about one and a half times their own height.

WHAT'S THE DIFFERENCE BETWEEN A RAINFOREST AND A JUNGLE?

Be honest, you thought they were the same thing, didn't you?

A rainforest is so called because of its climate: it rains a lot. To qualify as a rainforest, the annual rainfall needs to be at least 254 centimetres. But many jungles have a similarly damp climate. The main difference is that rainforests have lower light levels at ground level. The tall trees – around 30 metres high – let very little light through, so vegetation struggles to grow on the ground. That means it's not very difficult to walk through a rainforest and the canopy of trees blocks out wind and rain.

Jungles, on the other hand, have spaces between trees, letting more light through. Big plants can grow, so if you want to walk through a jungle, you'd better take something very sharp with you to cut through the dense vegetation.

Jungles often surround rainforests – as the trees become closer together, the jungle becomes a rainforest. Sometimes, jungles can be created out of rainforests if trees are cut or fall down.

Even though there are relatively few plants on a rainforest floor, the decomposing leaves and vines make it a haven for insects. Around 80% of all insect species live in rainforests.

SAVE THE RAINFORESTS,
SAVE THE WORLD

If rainforests continue to be destroyed at the current rate, there will be no rainforest left anywhere on Earth by 2040. 80% of the rainforest in Thailand has already been destroyed.

In the Amazonian rainforest alone, 2.5 million different insect species have been identified, as well as over 40,000 plant species, and 5,500 different species of mammals, fish, birds, reptiles and amphibians.

As well as tropical rainforests, such as the Amazonian rainforest or the Daintree rainforest in Australia, rainforests exist in colder parts of the world, as far north as Alaska.

WHAT'S THE DIFFERENCE BETWEEN POISONOUS AND VENOMOUS?

How many times have you heard people talk about 'poisonous snakes'? In fact, there's no such thing.

Poisonous plants will harm you if you eat or touch them. Poisonous creatures are the same – they contain poison, so you shouldn't eat or even touch them.

Venomous creatures have poison in them, too. The difference is that a venomous creature will inject its poison into you through its fangs or its sting.

TWO POISONOUS THINGS ...

● ● ● ● ● ● ● ● ● ● ● ● ● ● ● ● ● ●

OLEANDER

This flower might look good enough to eat, but don't – just one nibble could kill you.

PITOHUI AND IFRITA BIRDS

Papua New Guinea is home to both of these birds. They're the only poisonous birds in the world.

... AND TWO VENOMOUS THINGS

● ● ● ● ● ● ● ● ● ● ● ● ● ● ● ●

BLUE-RINGED OCTOPUS

When these little octopuses are angry, bright blue rings appear on their body. If you see them, swim away fast - they can paralyse and kill you with a single bite.

BLACK WIDOW SPIDERS

Black widows are famous for their venomous bites. But their deadly reputation isn't fair - it's rare for someone to die from a black widow bite.

KILLER CREATURES

In Japan, puffer fish, or fugu, is eaten as a delicacy. Specialist fugu chefs have to train for years to make sure they know how to remove the poisonous part of the fish, which is deadly if eaten. Deaths from fugu poisoning are very rare nowadays, and hardly ever result from restaurant-prepared fish – they're more likely to be people who have prepared puffer fish they've caught themselves. In the past deaths were more common: there were more than 150 in 1958!

The inland taipan snake, native to Australia, has the strongest venom of all snakes, but it's not the most deadly snake in the world – it lives in remote places, it isn't aggressive and it has shorter fangs than some other snakes, so it delivers less venom. The deadliest snake in the world – the one that kills more people than any other – is probably the carpet viper. It's found in Africa, Asia and the Middle East.

WHAT'S THE DIFFERENCE BETWEEN A DOLPHIN AND A PORPOISE?

How would you know whether you were swimming with dolphins or porpoises? And would it matter?

Dolphins and porpoises are both marine mammals. In fact, they're also both whales. They're also both toothed whales – unlike baleen whales that filter plankton through material called baleen on their upper jaw. But here's how to tell dolphins and porpoises apart:

Dolphins ...
... are likely to be longer and sleeker.
... have a pointed snout.
... have cone-shaped teeth.
... live in large groups.
... are found in temperate and tropical waters.

Porpoises ...
... are usually smaller than dolphins.
... have a blunt snout.
... have flat, spade-shaped teeth.
... live in groups of fewer than ten individuals.
... are found in temperate not tropical waters.

If you're wondering what you're swimming with, it's more likely to be a dolphin, because porpoises are much more shy. They're also less prone to leaping out of the water and other acrobatics.

Big friendly orcas ...

Orcas, also known as killer whales, are dolphins' and porpoises' big, scary cousins. They feed on large marine mammals such as penguins and seals, they're huge – 9 metres long and as heavy as an African elephant, have big teeth and are more than capable of eating a human being. But don't worry – it's extremely rare for an orca to attack a human. They also have an enormous fin on their backs – up to 1.8 metres high.

... and dolphins and porpoises

There are various reports of groups of dolphins protecting humans from sharks, by surrounding them and guiding them back to shore. The *Mary Poppins* actor, Dick Van Dyke, claimed that he drifted far out to sea after nodding off on his surfboard, and woke up to find himself being pushed back to the beach by a pod of friendly porpoises.

Extinct dolphins

Sadly, the Chinese river dolphin, or Baiji, was declared extinct in 2007. It was small and almost blind, with a very long, pointed snout, and only lived in the Yangtze River in China.

WHAT'S THE DIFFERENCE BETWEEN A METEOR AND A METEORITE?

Bad news for anyone confused about meteors and meteorites – it turns out there are meteoroids, too.

A meteor is a shooting star – the flash of light you see when a piece of space debris burns up as it falls through Earth's atmosphere. The actual piece of debris, which can be made of rock or metal, isn't called a meteor, but a meteoroid.

Usually, the meteoroid completely burns up before it reaches the Earth's surface. But a meteoroid that makes it all the way to Earth is called a meteorite. A meteorite can be the size of a pebble and weigh just a few grams, or it might be much larger, forming a whopping great crater as it smashes into the Earth. The biggest meteorite ever found fell in Namibia. It's the size of a truck and weighs 60 tonnes.

Asteroids and comets

Asteroids are bigger than meteoroids. They're chunks of rock or metal in orbit around the Sun – most of them are in the Asteroid belt between Mars and Jupiter.

Comets are like asteroids, but they're covered with ice, methane, ammonia and other substances that combine to form a shell around the rocky core. The shell is known as a coma, and sometimes it leaves a visible tail behind the comet when it travels close to the Sun. Comets orbit the Sun, too, but have longer, more egg-shaped orbits.

Direct hit

You'd have to be very unlucky to be hit by a meteorite, but it has been known to happen. In 1954 in Alabama, a 31-year-old woman was hit by a grapefruit-sized meteorite as she sat in her living room. She was bruised, but otherwise fine. The most recent case was in Uganda, where a young boy was hit by a small meteorite fragment only a few grams in weight. He wasn't hurt.

Fireball!

Meteoroids and other space debris sometimes enter Earth's atmosphere briefly and leave again, bouncing back out into space. They go by the wonderful name of Earth-grazing fireballs.

WHAT'S THE DIFFERENCE BETWEEN RUGBY LEAGUE AND RUGBY UNION?

They both use the same funny-shaped ball that players are allowed to pick up and run about with – and they're both called rugby. Surely that makes them the same thing?

When rugby was first played, during the 19th century, there was only one kind. But towards the end of the century, a split developed between teams whose players were paid to play (rugby league) and teams whose players weren't paid (rugby union). Today, professional rugby union players are paid, and both sports compete at national and international levels, but rugby union is much more common at international level – the Six Nations and the Rugby World Cup are both rugby union.

Over the years since the split was made, rugby league and rugby union developed different rules. In both games, the object is to score a 'try' by getting the ball over the other team's 'try line' near the end of the pitch. Players have to pass the ball backwards to their teammates (passing forwards isn't allowed), and matches are divided into two halves of forty minutes each. But there are lots of differences, too. Here are a few of the basic ones ...

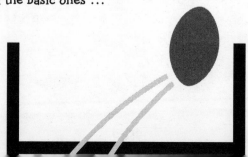

• The most obvious difference is the number of players: rugby union has fifteen, rugby league has thirteen.

• The size of the pitches are different – though the distance between try lines is the same for both: 100 metres.

• Tries, goals – scored by kicking the ball over the H-shaped post – and penalty goals are worth different amounts of points in each sport.

It all gets even more complicated than that, but if you're not sure which you're watching, count the number of players.

WHERE IT ALL BEGAN ... OR NOT

There's a story that rugby was invented in 1823, when a boy named William Webb Ellis picked up the ball during a game of football at Rugby School. There's no evidence to suggest that's what really happened, but the rugby world cup is called the William Webb Ellis trophy anyway.

WHAT'S THE DIFFERENCE BETWEEN A SWAMP AND A MARSH?

If you've ever been lost in soggy wetland, savaged by mosquitos, mysterious animal noises all around you and only a leaky canoe for protection, you've probably asked yourself this very question.

Swamps and marshes are both wet – as you already know. Both contain either salt water or fresh water, and both are home to plants and animals. The differences depend partly on which continent you're in ...

• In North America, a swamp differs from a marsh because it has a lot of trees in it – marshes have grasses and reeds.

• African swamps have a lot of papyrus rather than trees. Watch out, because they might have a lot of hippos, too.

• Generally, swamps contain greater areas of water with nothing growing in them than marshes do. Marsh water tends to have reeds and grass growing up through most of it.

Bogs and fens

BOGS are wetland areas with lots of peat in them – peat is soil made up mostly of decayed vegetation. Their water

108

comes from rainfall, rather than a river or water running down from higher ground. They're acidic, low in minerals and usually have a lot of moss but not much other plant life.

FENS are wetland areas, too, but the water comes from under the ground. They're much less acidic than bogs, rich in minerals, and contain a wide range of plants.

• •

ALLIGATOR AND CROC SPOT

The Florida Everglades is an area of a mix of swamps and marshes and is home to an enormous variety of plants and animals. It's the only place in the world where both alligators and crocodiles can be found (see page 62).

• •

Bog bodies

The cold acidic water and lack of oxygen in some bogs means that bodies can be preserved in them for thousands of years. Most of the human bog bodies that have been discovered are from the Iron Age, and they've been found in Britain, Ireland, Scandinavia, Germany and the Netherlands. Similarities between the bodies, such as evidence of violent deaths, suggest that they were killed and put into the bog in a ritual. Perhaps they were human sacrifices, or executions. The oldest bog body ever found, Koelbjerg Woman, dates from around ten thousand years ago, during the Stone Age.

WHAT'S THE DIFFERENCE BETWEEN RAVENS, CROWS, ROOKS AND JACKDAWS?

All of these birds are members of the crow family, Corvus. Here are some of the differences between them:

RAVENS are the largest member of the crow family. They're big – up to around 65 centimetres long, with a wingspan of 1.5 metres, which is probably wider than you are tall. They have black beaks and feathers.

ROOKS are black, too, but they have greyish-white faces and thinner beaks. They're the second largest member of the crow family – up to about 50 centimetres long with 1.2-metre wingspans.

The CROWS you're most likely to see around are carrion crows or hooded crows. They're both smaller than ravens at around 40 centimetres, with wingspans of up to about a metre. Carrion crows are black, and hooded crows have black heads, tails and wings, but their backs and breasts are grey.

JACKDAWS are the smallest crows. They're around 25 centimetres long, with wingspans of 50 centimetres. They have black heads with grey cheeks.

There are hundreds of other members of the crow family –
magpies and jays among them.

THE RAVENS AT THE TOWER

At least six ravens live at the Tower of London
at all times. There's a superstition that if
the six ravens leave the Tower, the kingdom
will fall. The Ravenmaster has the job of
looking after them, feeding them 170 grams of
raw meat every day, and bird biscuits soaked
in blood. They're kept in cages at night but
allowed out during the day. All of them have
names: the current seven (there's a spare)
are called Hardey, Thor, Odin, Gwyllum,
Cedric, Hugine and Munin.

Clever crows

One kind of crow, which lives on an island in the South
Pacific, is the only animal apart from apes and monkeys that
makes and uses tools in the wild. The crows peck at branches
to make hooks, and tear leaves into strips for poking food
out of difficult-to-reach places. Scientists studying the crows
have set them complicated problems, which the birds have
managed to solve.

WHAT'S THE DIFFERENCE BETWEEN A TIDAL WAVE AND A TSUNAMI?

Are they the same thing? Well, sort of. Tsunamis are often called 'tidal waves'. But a tidal wave is also another name for a tidal bore. So what's that, and what's the difference?

Tsunamis

Tsunamis have nothing to do with the sea's tides, so calling them 'tidal waves' is confusing. Tides are caused by the gravity of the Sun and the Moon pulling on the planet, but tsunamis are most often caused by undersea earthquakes.

A strong earthquake under the sea creates waves that travel for thousands of kilometres over the surface of the ocean. In deep water, the waves move at up to 800 kilometres per hour, but they are not very big – usually they're not even high enough to be noticed by ships as they pass. That's one of the reasons there isn't much warning of a coming tsunami.

But as the tsunami approaches the shore and the water becomes more shallow, the waves get higher and higher, and can be huge and powerful by the time they crash on to land. Unfortunately, people are often taken by surprise. Tsunamis can also be caused by landslides, and underwater explosions – and even by meteorites crashing into the sea (though this is very rare).

Tidal bores

Tidal bores ARE connected to tides. A tidal bore happens when the incoming tide pushes up a river and forms a wave that goes against the river's current. The wave could just be a ripple, but in some places it can be a huge, towering wave. Tidal bores happen in rivers all around the world.

TSUNAMI TRAGEDY

The most devastating tsunami in history happened on 26 December 2004, when an earthquake in the Indian Ocean triggered a massive tsunami that affected Indonesia, Sri Lanka, Thailand, India and the Maldives. Hundreds of thousands of people died.

WHAT'S THE DIFFERENCE BETWEEN A RAT AND A MOUSE?

You're sitting watching TV one night when you hear a scratching noise near the skirting board ... and the next day you notice a hole in your cereal box. Hang on, are those teeth marks? Aaarrgh! Something furry's scurrying across the kitchen floor!

You know you have a problem, but how bad is it? Is it a mouse – big problem – or a rat – really big problem: rats are even bigger and dirtier than mice?

It all depends on which type of rat and which type of mouse you're talking about. Rats are medium-sized rodents with long tails, and mice are small rodents with long tails. There are lots of species of rats and mice, and not all of them are closely related. For example, the naked mole rat, which lives underground and has tiny eyes, pale, furless skin and two very long front teeth, is completely different from the kangaroo rat, which has honey-coloured fur, large eyes, and bounces around like a kangaroo. But, millions of years ago, all rats and mice did have a common ancestor. The kinds of rat and mouse that often get into people's homes and gnaw your food packets, leaving little rodent footprints on your kitchen floor are brown rats, also known as Norwegian rats, and house mice.

The most obvious difference between brown rats and house mice is their size. Brown rats are bigger, longer and heavier than house mice. They weigh 350-650 grams, their bodies can measure up to about 25 centimetres, and their tails measure up to about 22 centimetres. House mice are smaller, shorter and lighter than brown rats. They weigh 30-90 grams, their bodies are up to 10 centimetres long, and their tails are up to 10 centimetres long. So if you spot one scuttling across the kitchen, it should be pretty easy to tell which kind of creature you're dealing with.

A baby rat and an adult mouse might be more difficult to tell apart though – they'll be pretty much the same size. Here are some pointers:

- **A baby rat's ears are smaller in relation to its head than an adult mouse's.**

- **An adult mouse's face is more pointed than a baby rat's.**

- **A baby rat's tail is thicker than an adult mouse's.**

- **A baby rat's head and its feet, especially the back ones, look large in relation to its body.**

- **An adult mouse's tail is about the same length as its body. A baby rat's tail is shorter.**

Rats and mice tend to come out only when it's dark and the lights are off, so you might not see them at all – but you will see evidence of them. The easiest way to tell whether you have mice or rats is the size of the droppings you'll probably see lying around. A rat's poo is a centimetre or more long, while mouse droppings are much smaller.

RAT STATS

Although a brown rat can be 25 centimetres long, it can squeeze through a gap just 1.5 centimetres wide. Brown rats can jump at least four times their own height, but they can't burp or vomit.

GOT TOOTHACHE? CHEW A MOUSE

In ancient Rome fillings were sometimes done with the ash from burnt mouse droppings, and some ancient Romans chewed mice twice a month to prevent toothache.

WHAT'S THE DIFFERENCE BETWEEN A PLANT AND AN ANIMAL?

It's obvious, isn't it? After all, you're quite different from an oak tree. But then again, what about a sea anemone – is that a plant, or an animal?

The differences between the different kingdoms of living things – plants, animals, fungus, algae and bacteria – aren't always obvious as you might think. Here are the most basic differences between plants and animals:

Plants can't move about – they are quite literally rooted to the spot. Some do move their heads to follow the Sun as it crosses the sky, and some carnivorous, or meat-eating, plants snap shut when an insect lands on them – but they can't go for walks.

Animals have mouths – they eat and drink to get the energy they need. Plant's don't – they use a process called photosynthesis to convert carbon dioxide in the atmosphere into energy to help them grow. Most plants take in water from the soil, using their roots. Carnivorous plants also get nutrients from the insects they trap, but they don't get energy from them, so it's not the same as eating.

The most basic difference between plants and animals is the structure of the cells that all living things are made of.

Plant cells have tough cell walls to protect them against things like wind and rain, but animal cells don't. And plant cells contain structures called chloroplasts, which capture light energy and help photosynthesis take place – they also make plants green.

So, what's a sea anemone? It's actually an animal – even though it looks like a plant and it's named after one (anemones are small woodland flowers). It can move about, it eats small animals, and it doesn't photosynthesize.

Resurrected plants

The resurrection plant can't walk, but it does move about: when there's a period of drought, it dries up, goes into a sort of sleeping state, and gets blown about by the wind. When it's watered again – which could be up to fifty years later – it comes back to life.

Smelly plants

What's the world's most stinky plant? There are two contenders for the title. The corpse flower smells like decaying flesh, and the flowers of the titam arum smell like rotting meat, too. Their stink attracts flies, which land on the flowers and pollinate the plants. Both plants produce enormous flowers – the titam arum can be up to three metres high!, so you can imagine how strong the stench is.

WHAT'S THE DIFFERENCE BETWEEN FOG AND MIST?

Have you ever wondered what it would be like to stand in the middle of a cloud? It turns out you've probably experienced something very similar. A cloud is just a lot of water droplets hanging close together in the sky, and that's what fog and mist are, too – they're just closer to the ground. The water droplets are microscopic – the closer together and larger the water droplets are, the thicker the mist (or fog, or cloud).

So if fog and mist are pretty much the same thing, is there any difference between them at all? Well, sort of, but it depends who you are and what you're doing ...

If you're flying a plane, mist is mist until you can't see further than 1,000 metres in front of you, then it officially becomes fog. Most weather reports use the 1,000 metres rule, too. But the UK have an extra definition – probably because the British are so fond of talking about the weather: if you're in the UK and you're walking or driving a car, it's fog when you can't see further than 200 metres in front of you.

Smoggy cities

London used to be famous for its 'smog'. The word is a combination of the words 'smoke' and fog' and it was caused mainly by smoke from coal fires. Smog even gave London its old nickname, 'The Smoke'. Not surprisingly, breathing in the smog was very bad for people's health. In the winter of 1952, thousands of people died as a result of the Great Smog, which lasted only four days. After that, laws were introduced to stop people burning so many coal fires.

Even today, big cities all over the world still get smog, produced by vehicle emissions and pollution from factories, and it's still a health hazard. Among the world's most polluted, smoggy cities are Mexico City in Mexico, Beijing in China, Buenos Aires in Argentina, Cairo in Egypt and Seoul in South Korea.

Foggy places

The world's foggiest place is Grand Banks, just off the island of Newfoundland, which is part of Canada. It gets so much fog because a cold current of air and a much warmer one meet there, creating water vapour when they come together.

If you're looking for somewhere foggy to live, Argentia in Newfoundland has more than 200 foggy days a year, and so does Point Reyes in California.

WHAT'S THE DIFFERENCE BETWEEN CURRANTS, RAISINS AND SULTANAS?

Do you suffer from dried fruit confusion? No wonder: even though they come in different packets in the supermarket, currants, raisins and sultanas are all really just raisins.

Raisins are dried grapes. You might think that they're made from red grapes, because of their brown colour, but they're not – they start off life as white grapes. A sultana is a particular variety of white grape, pale yellow in colour, and when they're dried, they're bigger and paler than ordinary raisins. Currants are made from red grapes, and they're the least sweet. They don't have anything to do with blackcurrants or redcurrants.

Just in case you were wondering about prunes – they're dried plums, so they're nothing to do with raisins at all.

LOO ALERT

Be warned: prunes are a natural laxative (they make you need to ... er ... go to the toilet, urgently), and so are other dried fruits, including dried apricots and dates.

WHAT'S THE DIFFERENCE BETWEEN A CODE AND A CIPHER?

● ● ● ● ● ● ● ● ● ● ● ● ● ● ● ● ● ●

You're dressed in your trenchcoat and trilby hat, reading a newspaper in the secret location. A man comes and puts a briefcase down next to you. 'The dead pigeon flies tonight,' he mutters. That's all very well, you think – but is that a code or a cipher? Or is he just being weird?

Some people use the words 'code' and 'cipher' as if they mean the same thing – but those people are sadly mistaken. A cipher substitutes numbers, symbols or other letters for each letter of a message – or mixes up the letters in the message. For example:

A	B	C	D	E	F	G	H	I	J	K	L	M
1	2	3	4	5	6	7	8	9	10	11	12	13

N	O	P	Q	R	S	T	U	V	W	X	Y	Z
14	15	16	17	18	19	20	21	22	23	24	25	26

Using this cipher, the word 'BAD' would be written as 214. Or you could move each letter in your message forward two letters in the alphabet, so that the word CUSTARD would be written EWUVCTF. You could also encipher CUSTARD by mixing the letters up, perhaps swapping over each pair, then grouping them differently: UCTS RAD. Though why someone would want to encipher the word 'custard' is anybody's guess.

A code, on the other hand, substitutes whole words or phrases with a different word, group of words or symbol. So, the word 'JELLY' might be the code word for 'DANGEROUS'. The phrase I LIKE CUSTARD could be a code for the phrase JONES IS A DOUBLE AGENT. You and the person you're sending the message to would have to work out the code beforehand – you might each need to have a codebook, because remembering all those words and phrases would be very difficult. In fact, maybe you'd want to encipher the code, just in case one of the code books fell into enemy hands. So perhaps THAT'S why someone might want to encipher the word 'custard'.

Codes can also be used to keep messages short as well as keeping them secret. If you have a mobile phone, you and your friends might already use a code like this when you're texting.

CODES

UNCRACKABLE CODE?

In the early 1900s, a rare book collector bought an old illustrated book, written in a strange language and alphabet, that became known as the Voynich Manuscript. It's thought to date from the 15th century. No one has ever been able to decipher it, but the pictures give clues: there are plants, stars and planets, the human body (possibly) and a calendar (possibly). Expert code-breakers have tried to make sense of the book, but no one has ever succeeded.

WHAT'S THE DIFFERENCE BETWEEN TURTLES, TERRAPINS AND TORTOISES?

They all have shells and look about a million years old – but what makes them different?

Turtles, terrapins and tortoises are all reptiles that belong to the turtle family. So tortoises and terrapins could be described as 'turtles', too. But actually, which is which depends on where you live

In the UK, tortoises are the shelled reptiles that walk on land. Turtles swim in the sea. Terrapins live in 'brackish' (slightly salty) or fresh water.

In the US, tortoises walk on land, turtles swim in fresh water, and sea turtles swim in the sea. But often the word 'turtle' is used for all three types of creature. Americans use the word 'terrapin' to describe one particular creature that lives in brackish water.

In Australia, our shelled friends are called turtles if they have front flippers and tortoises if they don't. The creatures British people call terrapins count as turtles in Australia because they have webbed feet.

TORTOISE AND TURTLE TRIVIA

Land tortoises are famously slow - they creep along at around 0.8 kilometres per hour, or km/h - only twice the speed of a snail. But turtles can swim very fast - the Loggerhead turtle has been clocked at around 35 km/h, which is the speed limit for cars at school rush hours.

Jellyfish are a turtle's favourite food. Unfortunately, they can mistake plastic bags floating in the sea for jellyfish, and eating those can kill them.

The largest turtle of all is the Leatherback turtle. It can be 1.8 metres long - your dad might be as tall as that - and weigh 540 kg - as much as a horse. It doesn't have an obvious shell like other turtles, but instead has bony plates on its back.

WHAT'S THE DIFFERENCE BETWEEN WEATHER AND CLIMATE?

What goes on in the atmosphere can burn your face or put an icicle on the end of your nose. But is that weather, or climate? Or both?

The difference between weather and climate is really time. Weather – the temperature, whether it's sunny, raining, foggy, humid or light-cloud-with-scattered-showers – is governed by the Earth's atmosphere and can change on a daily or hourly basis.

Climate is the word used to describe exactly the same things, but over a much longer time scale. It depends on averages of temperature, brightness, cloud, humidity, and so on, over a number of years. Different parts of the world have different climates. You might live in a hot, damp climate like a rainforest – or a dry, cold one, like Antarctica. You can also talk about the climate of the whole world, and whether it's generally getting hotter over a long period of time, which it is.

CLIMATE CHANGE CHALLENGE

People have got a lot to answer for. By burning huge amounts of fossil fuel, such as coal and oil, for cars, planes and power stations, we've released lots of carbon dioxide into the atmosphere. The extra carbon dioxide traps the heat from the Sun and makes the Earth hotter. The effects of climate change are already obvious: the ice at the north and south poles is beginning to melt, which is making sea levels rise and flooding low-lying land. The weather is likely to become more difficult to predict, with more violent storms. Now we've got to try and do something about it – and quickly. Perhaps you could help – maybe by inventing a new kind of pollution-free fuel.

WHAT'S THE DIFFERENCE BETWEEN GRIZZLY AND GRISLY?

Are bears grizzly or grisly – or both?

Grizzle means grey hair. So you could describe an old man as 'grizzled' (assuming he didn't mind). Grizzly bears are called grizzly because they often have white-tipped fur. The bears look brown, though, and you probably wouldn't want to get close enough to notice the white ends – if you did, you might die a grisly death.

Grisly means horrifying or revolting. So you might describe a rat's nest or a zombie as grisly. Or maybe even a grizzly bear ... which makes things a bit confusing.

Which word?

'Grisly' and 'grizzly' aren't the only words people get mixed up. Here are some others:

Effect

The result that something has. For example:
The teacher's droning voice had a sleep-inducing effect.
It can also be used as a verb, meaning to make or accomplish.

Affect

To influence. For example:
If you don't listen in class it will affect your exam results.

Compliment

Praise. For example:
I complimented her on her knitting skills.
It can also be used as a verb, to praise.

Complement

Something that completes. For example:
A glass of water is the best complement to a meal.
It can also be used as a verb, to complete.

Council

A group that leads, governs or advises. For example:
The local council has banned skateboarding.

Counsel

To advise. For example:

I would counsel you to stop skateboarding in the carpark.
It can be also used as a noun.

Imply
To suggest or hint. For example:
He implied I'd been cheating.

Infer
To reach an opinion based on statements or facts. For example:
I infer from these identical answers that students have cheated.

Its
Belonging to, or of, it. For example:
The dog chased its ball.

It's
It is. For example:
It's a golden retriever.

Principal
As an adjective: first, or most important. For example:
Chocolate is the principal ingredient of that cake.
As a noun: leader — for example, the principal actor or the principal of a school.

Principle
A general truth or law — it's always a noun, not an adjective. For example:
Do you know the basic principles of cookery?

WHAT'S THE DIFFERENCE BETWEEN TORNADOES, HURRICANES, TYPHOONS AND CYCLONES?

How many different types of violent wind can there be? And yes, we ARE just talking about the weather.

A tornado is an extremely powerful, whirling column of air. Tornadoes produce the fastest winds on earth (over 500 km/h) and they can be over 1.5 kilometres wide. As they travel along in an unpredictable path of spinning destruction, tornadoes pick up dust and debris, so they're visible as a funnel of swirling dust. They can easily pick up cars and even mobile homes. Almost all tornadoes happen in the United States.

Hurricanes are the most violent storms on Earth, with high winds, torrential rain, thunder and lightning. Although tornadoes spin at faster speeds, hurricanes are bigger and more powerful. They can measure as much as 500 kilometres across – the distance between Glasgow, in Scotland, and Oxford, in the south of England.

They sink ships, flatten buildings, smash vehicles, and bring down power lines, causing a lethal hazard with driving rain.

Hurricanes occur in tropical areas, close to the equator. To qualify as a hurricane, wind speed must be more than 120 km/h – enough to uproot a tree. If a storm's wind speed is below that, but above 63 km/h, it's called a tropical storm.

Hurricanes are called hurricanes if they happen in the Eastern and Central Pacific. In the Western Pacific they're known as typhoons. The word 'cyclone' can be used to describe hurricanes, typhoons and tropical storms.

Tornado tips

Most tornadoes aren't violent (only 2% are really powerful). They don't last very long, and weather forecasts should give plenty warning of their approach, although the path of a tornado is unpredictable. Avoid Oklahoma if you don't want to get caught up in one: it's the US state most likely to experience tornadoes.

Hurricane Hilda

Hurricanes are given names – Andrew, Betsy and Carmen, for example – following a system that has a name for most letters of the alphabet in six lists that rotate. If a hurricane is especially devastating, the name is retired from the list. So there won't be another hurricane Katrina, which happened in 2005, and is one of the deadliest hurricanes in history – it killed thousands of people and caused damage that cost billions of dollars to repair.

WHAT'S THE DIFFERENCE BETWEEN GRASSHOPPERS, CRICKETS AND LOCUSTS?

Which of these insects chirp at night, which chatted to *Pinocchio* in the Disney film, and which can form plagues of biblical proportions?

Grasshoppers, crickets and locusts are all members of the grasshopper family. They all of have powerful hind legs for jumping, make a chirping sound – called stridulation – and change from wingless young nymphs to adults with wings. But there are differences between them:

Grasshoppers and locusts ...
... are active during the day.
... make their chirping noise by scraping their back legs against their wings.
... have short antennae.
... eat plants – mainly grass.

Crickets ...
... are active at night.
... make their chirping noise by scraping their wings together.
... have long antennae – they can be several times as long as the body.
... sometimes prey on other creatures.

... and Jiminy Cricket was the talking insect in *Pinocchio*.

Plagues of locusts

When the locust population is fairly small, locusts behave just like other grasshoppers, living on their own, eating grass and minding their own business. But sometimes there's a population explosion, and when that happens, they behave differently, forming huge swarms. The locusts change colour, breed more, and eat much more than usual – each locust can consume its own body weight in a day. Swarms can number billions and spread over vast areas, munching crops and destroying farmers' livelihoods. In 2008, a swarm of locusts in Australia measured nearly six kilometres long!

HIGH HOPPERS

There are lots of different kinds of grasshopper. Some can fly and some can't, but they're all amazing leapers – they can jump up to 20 times the length of their own bodies.

WHAT'S THE DIFFERENCE BETWEEN A PSYCHIATRIST AND A PSYCHOLOGIST?

They're both doctors who deal with what goes on inside our heads. But they approach mental health problems in different ways ...

The main difference between psychiatrists and psychologists is that psychiatrists have a background in medicine, and psychologists don't. A psychiatrist has gone to medical school and studied to be the kind of doctor that treats physical problems. A psychologist has an advanced degree, known as a PhD, in psychology – the study of the human mind. But even though psychologists haven't studied medicine, they're still doctors. If you have a PhD in any subject, you get the title 'doctor'. But only doctors of medicine are able to prescribe drugs to help treat mental illness – so psychologists can't do that. They focus on therapy without drugs, by talking to people and trying to help them understand and change their behaviour.

Psychoanalysis

Psychoanalysis, a particular way of thinking about how our minds work and how to treat mental illness or distress, was developed by the psychologist Sigmund Freud in the late 19th and early 20th centuries. Freud was the first person to suggest that people have thoughts and wishes that they're not aware of in their conscious minds.

137

BRILLIANT BRAINS

The cerebral cortex is the largest area of the brain and we use it to think, remember and sense things around us. But we still don't know how it works. There are around 15 billion brain cells in the cerebral cortex, which are constantly connecting with one another and changing - hundreds of times a second. So perhaps it's not surprising that it's difficult to study this bit of our brains.

There's a brain museum in Lima, Peru, which has a collection of nearly 3,000 human brains. The museum is open to the public, but the largest collection of human brains in the world - Harvard Tissue Resource Center - isn't. It holds around 6,700 brains.

Different parts of the brain specialize in particular things. There's an area that deals with remembering names, another recognizes people's face, another forms new memories involving times and places. There's even a part of the brain devoted to sneezing.

WHAT'S THE DIFFERENCE BETWEEN SLEET, HAIL AND FREEZING RAIN?

If you live in Britain, you'll probably be familiar with these weather conditions. Sleet, hail and freezing rain can all ruin a day out. But do you have any idea what they actually are?

Freezing rain falls as a liquid but freezes when it hits cold surfaces that are at freezing point or just below it. Often, it begins falling as snow, then hits a layer of warmer air that makes it melt. So it looks just like ordinary rain, but freezes into ice when it hits a frozen car windscreen. And it feels very, very cold indeed when it hits you on the nose. Freezing rain can be very dangerous, especially because people often assume there can't be any ice about because it's raining.

If you're British or Australian, you'll use the word 'sleet' to describe very wet, slushy snow. In North America, sleet is made up of frozen raindrops that bounce when they hit the ground – in other words, what British or Australian people would describe as hail.

Hail is formed in violent thunderstorms when water freezes on to snowflakes and forms pellets of ice, which are larger than the frozen raindrops that Brits and Australians also call 'hail'. Sometimes the pellets reach the bottom of the cloud and are pushed back to the top by a strong upward blast of air, where they are coated with another layer of ice – and this can happen several times, forming great big lumps that eventually fall to the ground. Hail can cause a lot of damage.

Giant hail:

Hailstones can reach gigantic proportions: the biggest ever recorded was 20 centimetres in diameter (not much smaller than a football!), weighed 880 grams and fell in South Dakota, USA, in 2010.

Insane rain:

If you think giant hail is alarming, there have been cases of far more unusual things raining from the sky. In Jennings, Louisiana in 2007, there was a rain of worms, and in the same year, fish rained down on Paracatu in Brazil. In 2010, there was another fish rainfall, this time in Lajamanu, Australia. And in Honduras, rains of fish are commonplace — one or two per year have been reported over the last 100 years, and there's a Festival of the Rain of Fishes celebrated every year in the city of Yoro in Honduras. Various other animals — including jellyfish, squid and birds — have been reported falling from the sky. One theory is that the creatures are picked up in waterspouts — tornadoes out at sea — and whirled through the atmosphere before being deposited, sometimes frozen and most often dead, over land.

WHAT'S THE DIFFERENCE BETWEEN A HEADACHE AND A MIGRAINE?

Is a migraine just a dramatic-sounding word for a bad headache?

A migraine is a bad headache, but it's not just a bad headache. There are several stages to a migraine - though sufferers might not all experience all of them. If you're one of the unlucky people who get migraines, you might:

• have aches and pains, feel grumpy, or lose your appetite for a few hours or days before a migraine. This is known as the 'prodromal stage'.

• see flashing lights before a migraine begins, for between 15 and 60 minutes. About a third of migraine sufferers experience this, which is called the 'aura stage'.

• you'll definitely get a headache. It's really nasty and it's usually a throbbing pain on one side of your head. You might feel sick, or even be sick, and need to stay away from bright light and loud noise. The headache can last between four hours and three whole agonizing days.

• after the headache, you might feel very tired and weak, sometimes for several days. This is called the 'resolution stage'.

There isn't a cure for migraines, but they can be treated with painkillers and other drugs. There are lots of different types of headache, but its rare for other kinds to be as painful as a migraine headache.

STRANGE HEADACHE CURES

Here are some ways people tried to get rid of their headaches in the past ... they must have been desperate. Even if you're in agony, don't try any of these at home:

- Carry a nut in your pocket and keep stroking it.

- Tie a live frog to your head. Keep it there until it dies.

- Sprinkle a handful of salt on your head.

- Tie rags soaked in vinegar around your head.

- Apply sliced onion, or dust from the threshold of the door, to your forehead.

- Dip your hand in cold water, rub it on your head, then shake your hand dry.

- Wear rattlesnake rattles in your hat. Or just wrap a dead snake around your head.

- Tie a hangman's noose around your head.

- Get someone to blow tobacco smoke into each of your ears.

- Place a lock of your hair under a stone, or bury a lock of hair in the ground.

- Make up a bandage with slices of potatoes dipped in vinegar and tie it to your head.

WHAT'S THE DIFFERENCE BETWEEN A NEWT AND A SALAMANDER?

You might have seen one of these in a pond ... or was it a lake? But how can you tell if it was a newt or a salamander?

There are more than 500 species of salamander. They look like lizards, but they're not. They don't have scales, and in fact they're amphibians – cold-blooded, soft-skinned creatures, such as frogs and toads, which breathe water when they're young, and air when they're adults.

Newts are a kind of salamander. The main things that make newts different from other salamanders are their skin and tails. Newts usually have rougher skin than salamanders, which tend to be slimier, and newts have flatter tails.

But people call different species newts and salamanders, depending on whether they're from North America, Europe or Australia. So, to be on the safe side, call them all salamanders.

146

SALAMANDER STATS

The smallest salamanders are less than 3 centimetres long, but the biggest, the Chinese giant salamander, can be 1.8 metres long and weigh 65 kilograms - that's the size of a tall adult!

NEVER KISS A SALAMANDER: many produce poisonous secretions on their skin. In fact, it's not a good idea to touch them either.

Salamanders are the only vertebrates - animals with a backbone - that can regenerate their limbs, eyes, hearts, intestines and jaws. That means they can actually grow new ones. Wow - and urrggh!

WHAT'S THE DIFFERENCE BETWEEN A CANOE AND A KAYAK?

'Canoe' tell the difference between these two?

Canoes and kayaks are both small, narrow boats that are powered through the water by a person – or more than one person – paddling them. The main difference is the paddle: canoes are paddled with a single-bladed paddle – that is, the broad, flat bit is only on one end – while kayak paddles have two blades, one on each end. So, when you're paddling a canoe you need to swap sides with every stroke of the paddle – unless you want to go round in a circle – and when you're paddling a kayak you don't.

Canoes and kayaks can be either for one or two people, and canoes can be built to take more. Canoes usually have an open top, while kayaks are enclosed, but this isn't always the case. If in doubt, look at the paddle.

PADDLING INTO THE PAST

The oldest canoe ever discovered was found in Pesse, in the Netherlands. It's at least 9,500 years old.

For thousands of years, people hunted bowhead whales in the Arctic from small kayaks made out of walrus skin.

Some of the oldest canoes are made from hollowed-out tree trunks - and people still make canoes this way.

In 14th century Africa, tribes fought wars from canoes.

WHAT'S THE DIFFERENCE BETWEEN STALACTITES AND STALAGMITES?

They're both formations found inside caves, and one grows up and the other hangs down – but which is which?

Stalactites and stalagmites are formed by water seeping through cracks in the rock. Minerals in the water are released when they come into contact with the air in a cave. The minerals form solid deposits – either hanging from the ceiling, as the water drips down, or growing up from the floor, as the water splashes on the floor. A stalactite hangs from a cave ceiling, while a stalagmite grows up from the cave floor.

Here are two ways to remember which is which:

- A stalactite has to hang on tight to the ceiling, while a stalagmite might one day reach the cave ceiling.

- Tights hang down, mites grow up.

CURIOUS CAVES

Cave formations – or speleothems if you want to sound clever – are made over thousands of years. There are different types of stalagmites and stalactites, and their names sometimes tell you what they look like: there are broomstick stalagmites, fried egg stalagmites and soda straw stalactites. Sometimes a stalactite and a stalagmite growing towards one another meet and form a column.

There are other strange looking cave formations, too:

Cave pearls are very rare. They look similar to the pearls found in oyster shells, and are formed in a similar way – calcium salts form around a grain of sand or grit in a cave pool. They're usually spheres, like oyster shell pearls, but they can also be cylinders or even cubes.

Moonmilk is a gooey white substance made of fine crystals that doesn't harden. No one knows exactly how it's formed. An entire river of moonmilk, 150 metres long, was found in a Spanish cave in 2004.

Snottites are gooey, dripping bacteria colonies that hang from the rooves of sulfur caves, where conditions are hot, dark and extremely acidic.

WHAT'S THE DIFFERENCE BETWEEN A GAME AND A SPORT?

Some people get very angry about this, probably because 'sports' are taken more seriously than 'games'. But no one can really agree what the differences are.

Here are some of the many definitions that have been put forward:

A sport requires people to be physically there and participating, while a game doesn't.
You can use the internet to play a game of chess or ludo against someone on the other side of the world, but to play football, tennis or hockey you actually have to be there, flinging yourself about the pitch or court. By this definition, snooker and darts are both sports.

Players have to be constantly moving from beginning to end of the match or game, with no time out for thinking or planning the next move.
This would make darts and snooker both games.

Sport needs to be physically demanding.
It's only a sport if, as with tennis or rugby, you break a sweat when you're playing it. Otherwise – as in snooker or darts – it's a game.

A sport has to have a useful purpose.

That would make fishing, sprinting, driving a racing car and shooting all sports. Not all of these would involve you breaking into a sweat, of course. And by this definition, tennis, basketball, baseball, and so on, would all be games.

Sports have governing bodies – like the Football Association – and rules, and involve competition.

This would mean that things like Scrabble counted as sports.

But if you really like playing something and you consider it to be a sport rather than a game, why not make up your own definition?

• •

STRANGE SPORTS

Extreme accounting: players take part in perilous activities such as sky-diving, pot-holing or mountain-climbing, while balancing spreadsheets or completing audits at the same time. Extreme ironing, for daredevils who hate creased clothing, is another alternative.

Chessboxing: just like chess ... except, in between moves, both players enter a boxing ring and try to bash one another senseless.

Bog-snorkelling: competitors race through a 55-metre course marked out in a bog. There's an annual championship held every year in Powys, Wales. Players might also want to try bog-mountain-biking.

Stinging-nettle eating: a world championship competition is held every year in Dorset. Hang on, though – can this really be called a sport or a game? Isn't it just a contest? And what's the difference between a contest and a game? Maybe we shouldn't go there ...

Breathtaking game

In Bangladesh, the national game is kabaddi. Two teams take turns to send raiders into the opposing side, to tag or wrestle as many players as they can in a given amount of time. The twist is that the raiding players have to hold their breath for the whole time they are in the opposing team's territory, muttering 'kabaddi, kabaddi, kabaddi' under their breath continuously to prove they're not cheating.

Synchronized scrabble

In Singapore in 2006, 1042 people played 521 games of Scrabble at the same time to create a world record for the most simultaneous Scrabble games.

TV Starcraft

Starcraft, the science-fiction strategy computer game, is so popular in Korea that professional teams play one another in televised tournaments.

WHAT'S THE DIFFERENCE BETWEEN A MOSQUITO AND A GNAT?

Did you just hear a high-pitched whining in your ear? Grab a fly-swat, just to be on the safe side, as you read on ...

'Mosquito' is the Spanish word for 'little fly', which is a pretty accurate description: they're small, flying, two-winged insects. Male mosquitoes feed on nectar but females need to feed on blood as well so that they can produce eggs. There are more than 2,500 different species of mosquito, some of them feed on human blood, and particular types can spread life-threatening diseases such as malaria, dengue fever and yellow fever.

The word 'gnat' isn't so easily defined. It's often used to describe mosquitoes, too, but all small, biting insects, such as sand flies and black flies, are commonly referred to as gnats, especially in Britain. Either way, they're all really annoying, and some of them are very dangerous indeed.

Malaria

Only one type of mosquito, the Anopheles, causes malaria. It carries a parasite that can be passed to humans via the mosquito's bite and causes the disease. Malaria kills more than a million people every year, mostly in Africa. As long as you're diagnosed with malaria early enough, and given the right medicine, you're unlikely to die.

ULTIMATE INSECTS

The world's largest flying insect ever discovered was the Meganeura. It looked a lot like a modern dragonfly, but it had a wingspan of a whopping 75 centimetres. It lived around 300 million years ago, before the Age of the Dinosaurs.

The biggest flying insect around today is probably the Hercules moth, which has a wingspan of around 27 centimetres.

The desert locust has the fastest airspeed of any flying insect: around 30 km/h. There are lots of other contenders for fastest flying insect, including dragonflies, and it's said that horseflies can reach speeds of 145 km/h!

WHAT'S THE DIFFERENCE BETWEEN LESS AND FEWER?

Some people get very grumpy about grammar. If you're one of them, you'll already know the answer to this question ...

Less and fewer don't mean the same thing. Oh no! 'Less' means 'not as much', and 'fewer' means 'not as many'. So if you drink some lemonade, you'll have less of it, and if you munch some sandwiches you'll have fewer of them.

So, if you can count something, such as countries, socks or pencils, there are fewer – and if you can't count something, such as jelly, enthusiasm or water, there are 'less'.

Here are a few examples of less and fewer in action:

- Fewer people
- Less congestion
- Fewer polar bears
- Less ice
- Fewer ice cubes
- Less orange squash
- Fewer oranges
- Less food

... you get the idea.

WHAT'S THE DIFFERENCE BETWEEN A PARROT, A MACAW AND A COCKATOO?

Parrots, macaws and cockatoos can all be trained to talk. But there's no point in asking them to explain why they're different from each other – they'll probably just shout rude words at you.

Parrots, macaws and cockatoos all belong to the same group of birds, called 'Psittaciformes' in Latin, with a silent 'p'. Macaws are a type of large parrot, which are found in most warmer parts of the world. Lorikeets and lovebirds are types of parrot, too.

Cockatoos, which are found in the Philippines, New Guinea, the Solomon Islands and Australia, tend to be bigger and less colourful than parrots. These are the other main differences between these chatty birds:

• **Cockatoos** have head crests, which they raise and lower to communicate with one another.

• **Cockatoos'** beaks are different from parrots': a cockatoo bite is likely to be worse than a parrot's bite, because its beak comes together in two separate places.

• **Parrots** are generally better at mimicking human speech than cockatoos, so if you're chatting away to something feathery, it's probably a parrot.

English parrots

If you go to London, Surrey and Kent, keep an ear out for squawking, and an eye out for a flash of green. If you see a bright green bird with a red beak, you've spotted a ring-necked parakeet, Britain's only wild parrot. They originally come from India and Africa, and no one is quite sure how they got to England, but there are now thousands of them. Some people think they're descended from escaped pets, and others think they were set free from a film studio.

Talking parrots

Pet parrots are often trained to talk. The most remarkable talking parrot was Alex, the subject of a 30-year experiment by an animal psychologist. Alex, who died in 2007, had a vocabulary of 150 words and could use it to correctly answer questions or ask them, and could even count up to six.

160

WHAT'S THE DIFFERENCE BETWEEN GENGHIS KHAN AND KUBLAI KHAN?

Are these rampaging rulers related, or do they just have the same last name? Well, it turns out 'Khan' wasn't really their last name at all ...

Genghis Khan was born in Mongolia in 1155 (or 1162 – no one is sure) with the name Borjigin Temujin. He rose to become khan, or leader, of a huge Mongol army. Genghis Khan, as he came to be known, means Universal Leader (he was a very modest type). With his terrifying hordes of heavily armed, deadly horsemen, Genghis conquered a massive empire, which stretched across Asia and eastern Europe.

After Genghis Khan died, in 1227, his empire grew even bigger. The Mongol empire was the largest continuous empire the world has ever known, and the second largest ever – the biggest was the British Empire, but that was scattered about the world, not in one large area like Genghis's.

Kublai Khan was Genghis Khan's grandson. He ruled from 1260, and extended the empire further, from China to Iraq and Siberia to Afghanistan, until he ruled a fifth of all the land in the world. In Europe, Kublai Khan is famous as the great leader who welcomed the Venetian explorer Marco Polo to China. Polo's epic journey to China lasted 24 years. Kublai Khan has become famous for his luxurious palace and court – a famous poem by Samuel Taylor Coleridge talks about Kublai Khan's 'stately pleasure-dome', but above all else he was fierce and successful conqueror, just like his granddad, Genghis.

ENORMOUS EMPIRES

These are the five biggest empires in history:
1. The British Empire – over 33 million km^2 in 1923.
2. The Mongol Empire – 33 million km^2 at the end of the 13th century.
3. The Russian Empire – 23 million km^2 in 1866.
4. The Spanish Empire – 20 million km^2 in the mid- to late-18th century.
5. The Qing Empire – 14 million km^2 at the end of the 18th century.

GHOSTLY GRAVE

Genghis Khan was buried in an unmarked grave, which has never been discovered. Genghis Khan wanted its location kept a secret, so it wouldn't be raided. Legend has it that soldiers accompanying the funeral escort killed anyone who crossed their path. The slaves who dug the grave were killed, and finally the soldiers themselves were killed – presumably by top-ranking army generals who were trusted to keep the secret. One story says that a river was diverted to hide the grave, to make absolutely sure it was never found.

WHAT'S THE DIFFERENCE BETWEEN SEALS AND SEA LIONS?

They're both furry marine mammals, but would you know which is which?

Seals and sea lions are closely related – they're in the same family group, 'Pinnipedia' in Latin, which also includes walruses. But there are some big differences between them:

SEALS ...

... don't have outer ears – they just have ear holes.
... have small, weak, furry front flippers.
... tend to be fatter than sea lions.
... are not as good as getting around on land as their sea lion cousins.

SEA LIONS ...

... have ear flaps you can see on either side of their heads – they are also known as 'eared seals'.
... have big, strong, hairless front flippers that they can stand up on.
... tend to be sleeker than seals.
... can rotate their hind flippers, which means they can get about very easily on land.
... are noisier than seals, making a loud, barking sound.

Just to confuse you, fur seals are very similar to sea lions, and share all the sea lion characteristics above.

Sea lions and seals are extremely good divers. The best diver of all is the elephant seal, which can dive as deep as 1,500 metres!

TUSK, TUSK

Walruses, which live in Arctic regions, are also related to seals and sea lions. They are enormous - they weigh up to 2,000 kilograms - nearly as much as a hippo. They have huge ivory tusks surrounded by whiskers. The tusks are up to a metre long and walruses use them to haul themselves out of the water and to make holes in the ice. Walrus tusks, and walrus oil and meat, made them so attractive to human hunters in the 18th and 19th centuries that walruses were wiped out in some places.

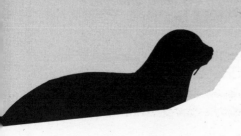

WHAT'S THE DIFFERENCE BETWEEN SNOT AND BOGEYS?

It's a question that's perplexed anyone who has ever picked their nose ...

As you might have guessed, the words 'snot' and 'bogey' do not feature in many medical dictionaries. Snot, or 'nasal mucus' if you want to get technical, is the slimy stuff that runs out of your nose when you have a cold. A bogey, on the other hand – or should we say 'hardened nasal mucus' – is a lump of snot that has dried out. It might be clinging to the inside of your nostril or – embarrassingly – stuck to the outside of your nose. For some people (naming no names), the essential characteristic of a bogey is that it can be flicked. Or eaten.

You'll probably agree that correct grammar is important in these cases, so you have 'less' snot, but 'fewer' bogeys (see page 158 for more about less and fewer).

WARNING: NOSE-PICKING CAN DAMAGE YOUR HEALTH

The word rhinotillexomania means excessive nose picking. Some people are compulsive nose-pickers and stay that way even once they've grown up. People who have rhinotillexomania can sometimes do their noses serious harm.

167

WHAT'S THE DIFFERENCE BETWEEN A WARLOCK AND A WIZARD?

You know how it is: you're popping along to the local coven for a get-together around the cauldron when suddenly you realize you don't know the difference between a wizard and a warlock – this could be very embarrassing. You need to find out the answers, and quickly.

Unfortunately, you're not going to find out anything absolutely definite. Or even slightly definitely, really. In folklore, both wizards and warlocks are magical beings, but there's no firm definition of either one – because folklore doesn't have long lists of rules and definitions. Some people think of a warlock as a male witch, while a wizard is more powerful – and they can both be good or bad. To others, a warlock is evil, dealing in black magic and all kinds of nastiness, while a wizard is good, like Gandalf in *The Lord of the Rings*, righting the wrongs of Middle Earth.

The origins of the words 'warlock' and 'wizard' give clues to why warlocks might be seen as baddies and wizards as goodies. 'Warlock' comes from a very old English word, meaning 'oath breaker'. Anyone who breaks a promise is clearly a very nasty piece of work. The word 'wizard', on the other hand, comes from a medieval word meaning 'wise' – and it's hard to be wise and an absolute rotter at the same time.

Warlocks and wizards do have one thing in common, though: neither of them exists. So if you think you're chatting to one, you might want to pinch yourself to see if you're dreaming ...

A Short Guide to Folktale Characters:

Troll: Like a human, but uglier, bigger and stronger, trolls are found lurking under bridges or in caves. They like to eat goats.

Ogre: Huge, aggressive and highly dangerous: ogres are giants capable of eating people.

Witch: Older women in pointy hats who cast spells around cauldrons and fly about on broomsticks. They are fond of cats.

Goblin: Small, mischievous people, sometimes hairy with or without outsized ears. Their business is making trouble for humans.

Hobgoblin: Like goblins, but kinder and with a sense of humour.

The gory Wizard of Oz

The Wizard of Oz is one of the world's most famous wizards – he first appeared in a children's novel by L. Frank Baum in 1900, and the book was made into a film in 1939 – and it's still popular more than 70 years later. The film company got rid of some of the gory bits in the book, such as bees stinging themselves to death, and wolves and a wildcat having their

WHAT'S THE DIFFERENCE BETWEEN ASTRONOMY AND ASTROLOGY?

Much to the annoyance of professors of astrophysics, people do sometimes get these very different things confused. However, if you go back in time far enough, you'll find they used to be quite similar.

Astronomy is the study of the universe outside the Earth's atmosphere. It tries to describe what's happening in space, and to explain how the universe formed and what will happen to it in the future. Thanks to astronomy, scientists can accurately plan spacecraft flights, and predict eclipses, comets, and more everyday things like the times of sunsets and sunrises.

Astrology uses the twelve signs of the Zodiac – the twelve constellations that the Sun passes through in one year – and claims to be able to predict what will happen to people based on the time and place of their birth. You might find an astrological horoscope page in a newspaper or magazine, telling you something like, 'If you're a Gemini, a friend will let you into a secret today!' or, 'Librans should watch out: someone could be out to betray you this week!'

The ancient Babylonians were the first people to identify the signs of the Zodiac, and they were also the first to name the stars and planets and use maths to predict their movements. They believed that the planets were ruled by gods, and that what went on in space affected the lives of humans. For them there wasn't a difference between astronomy and astrology at all.

Wobbly astrology

Since the days of the Babylonians, the Earth has shifted slightly on its axis, so that the Sun passes through the constellations in different months from the traditional dates for zodiac signs. You might think you're a Taurus, but you might really have been born when the Sun was passing through the constellation of Aries. The introduction of a thirteenth sign of the zodiac, Ophiucus – represented by a man carrying a large snake – has been suggested to put things right.

WHAT'S THE DIFFERENCE BETWEEN THE END AND THE CONCLUSION?

In this case, not much. A conclusion can just mean the same thing as an end, or it can mean a summing-up of what's gone before ...

So, here goes: in this book you've found out how to tell a frog from a toad, a hurricane from a tornado, and a wizard from a warlock (or not, as the case may be). That's probably exactly the sort of thing you were expecting, but who knew you'd also discover what ancient Romans did with mice, and why you might want to tie a rattlesnake to your hat. Hopefully, the next time someone asks you, 'What's the difference between poisonous and venomous?' you'll be able to tell them.